Rethinking Classroom Design

Rethinking Classroom Design

Create Student-Centered Learning Spaces for 6th–12th Graders

Todd Finley and Blake Wiggs

ROWMAN & LITTLEFIELD
Lanham • Boulder • New York • London

Published by Rowman & Littlefield
A wholly owned subsidiary of The Rowman & Littlefield Publishing Group, Inc.
4501 Forbes Boulevard, Suite 200, Lanham, Maryland 20706
www.rowman.com

Unit A, Whitacre Mews, 26-34 Stannary Street, London SE11 4AB

British Library Cataloguing in Publication Information Available

Library of Congress Cataloging-in-Publication Data
Names: Finley, Todd, author. | Wiggs, Blake, author.
Title: Rethinking classroom design : create student-centered learning spaces
    for 6th–12th graders / by Todd Finley and Blake Wiggs.
Description: Lanham : Rowman & Littlefield [2016] | Includes bibliographical references
    and index.
Identifiers: LCCN 2015040978| ISBN 9781475818529 (cloth : alk. paper) |
    ISBN 9781475818536 (pbk. : alk. paper) | ISBN 9781475818543 (electronic)
Subjects: LCSH: Classrooms—Planning. | Classroom environment.
Classification: LCC LB3325.C5 F56 2016 | DDC 371.6/2—dc23
LC record available at http://lccn.loc.gov/2015040978

♾™ The paper used in this publication meets the minimum requirements of American National Standard for Information Sciences—Permanence of Paper for Printed Library Materials, ANSI/NISO Z39.48-1992.

Printed in the United States of America

Todd's Dedication:
To my enchanting wife, Randi, who has socialized me into something approximating a human being.

Blake's Dedication:
To my patient wife, Jenn, who challenges me to live in the moment.

Contents

Foreword

This is a book about classroom design. As director at TeachThought, I sometimes work with the George Lucas Foundation and Edutopia.

Big Rock Ranch, Edutopia's headquarters, is nestled at the bottom of a massive, gray hill covered in white grass. Looking from left to right, you recognize that the hill isn't one thing, but a number of things: One hill is really a stretch of hills that becomes a kind of spine that encircles the ranch and makes you feel insignificant and surreal. It is perfect and serene and has orange dragonflies that move around in absolute silence, and at night you can look up and see geometry across and between the stars. This is where I met one of the book's authors, Todd Finley, also an Edutopia blogger.

Big Rock Ranch is a short drive from Skywalker Ranch, which we also visited, and also props itself up on design—the buildings here are laid out so that one can't be seen from another. Between these two spaces, the natural meets the synthetic with a kind of congruity that's quietly beautiful.

Design is everything. Or this time with less hyperbole, everything is a matter of design. Everything that is a *thing* features design elements, or is created and changed by sequences, systems, and other infrastructure *designed* around it.

Whether through an architect's eye, a farmer's hands, or the slow genius of evolution, both synthetic and natural *things* are a matter of craft and craftsmanship. They are observed, used, adapted, and used again to see how *this thing* in *this place* and this context works.

Let's move to education for more tidy analogies. As a middle and high school English teacher, I tried to help students see that the reading and writing of literature was a matter of design. That, in fact, English Language Arts as a class or content area is *The Art and Science of Media Design*. People have ideas to express (what they're saying), and a manner of expressing it (how they say it).

The *what* is the message, and the *how* is form, and both are matters of design. They are interoperational and interdependent and interfacing. They can't exist without one another. Even as digital technologies change modalities, patterns persist. Purpose, form, and audience all kind of meld together to get us close to the idea of design. Think of the disparities of form and theme across literary history.

Gilgamesh.
Homer's *Odyssey.*
Shakespeare's sonnets.
Fairy tales (e.g., Grimm's collections)
Lincoln's "Gettysburg Address"
Kerouac's *On the Road.*
Public Enemy's *Fight the Power.*
Wendell Berry's *What Are People For?*

Design isn't singular either. It's whole and inclusive. Each one of these works was meticulously crafted by someone moved to communicate an idea, that idea only relevant in a context we have to work hard to imagine it without. The world without that idea is impossible to imagine, as is the idea without the form, and the form without the design.

A Shakespearean sonnet that doesn't end in a neat couplet is something else.

Grimm's Fairy Tales cleansed of their tone and mood end up being Disney movies. *On the Road* organized into paragraphs and chapters becomes more of a distracted autobiography.

David Foster Wallace without the footnotes. Emily Dickinson without the em-dash. Frost without the math and meter. 2pac without his constant contradictions. A *Brave New World* without Mustapha Mond's rambling monologue at the end.

Without these things, they're *not* these things.

And so, your classroom. Steve Jobs designed fonts and iPods and iPhones and iPads, and as a professional in education, you're told to consider design in the same way. Of curriculum, units, lessons, and instruction you consider two of the core tenets of design, *audience* and *purpose*. Who needs to do what? Or more precisely, who needs to learn what?

And where does the learning happen? A classroom? Only the classroom? Don't learning spaces precede—or at least interface with—curriculum, units, lessons, and instruction? Isn't there an ecology here? Can you consider one thing without the other? Does it make sense to create a classroom seating chart without considering the learning model you're going to use? In this idea—that's where this book does its work.

By reading a book about classroom design—this book about classroom design—you have a chance to organize your teaching in a way that supports all of the other professional development and reading and twittering and reflection you do.

First, the micro—your classroom. The book is written for the teachers of today and tomorrow. In light of its simple and easy-to-follow organization, this book is for a practicing teacher interested in thinking strategically about the spaces used for teaching and learning. It can be skimmed or read more deeply, with an eye for utility. (There is an entire chapter about the teacher's desk—just the desk and how it might be used!)

It takes an itemized approach, looking first at the process of classroom design, then at the parts of a room (the pieces through which design occurs). This survey starts with bulletin boards (the second teacher), moves to student seating arrangements, and then moves swiftly into digital spaces where students and teachers interact, back to the physical classroom (i.e., the teacher's desk), and then ends, appropriately, with the ultimate output of all of this design: student work.

Then, the macro—learning contexts and spaces. Historically, education thinks in terms of books and desks and walls (which this book does as well), but chapters on blended learning—through learning management systems and assorted apps—mark a trend in classroom design that doesn't involve classrooms at all. Evernote, Dropbox, Google Classroom, and other digital resources both mimic and "push back on" schools and the square rooms that reside within them in a way that both serves and expands our collective vision for teaching.

That it begins with the process of design and ends with student work is itself a matter of design. This pattern of micro-to-macro thinking is a theme of *making things*, whether by authors or by designers or by teachers or by those who do all three. And this book is a thing and each chapter is a thing and your classroom is a thing and they all work together.

Your Google Drive and your grading system and state testing—they all have a relationship, yes? And your own sense of what a teacher is, and what your students need from you—these facets all interface daily in your classroom, whether by accident or by design.

Let your classroom be your greatest design.

—Terry Heick
Director at TeachThought

Acknowledgments

We are humbled by the generosity of so many people who helped this book come to fruition. Rowman & Littlefield's Sarah Jubar was our nimble superstar editor. We love her! Others helped with late-stage triage: wise Kerri Flinchbaugh, detail maniac Joanne Marks, heroic David Webb, bearded Phil Adams, lovely Terri Van Sickle, generous Adam Johnson, Doc Savage–like Brian Sztabnik, tech wonderkid Mark Samberg, and big-hearted Ruth Arseneault. You all helped us birth a book!

We would also like to thank enthusiastic Sonja McKay at Exploris and everyone who opened their classroom doors for this project. Also, many thanks to Jason Korreck and William Burgess for sharing their classroom photos.

Chapter 1

The Classroom Design Process

You cannot hold a design in your hand. It is not a thing. It is a process. A system. A way of thinking.

—B. Gill

Guiding Questions

- What is design thinking and why does it matter?
- How can I involve my students in redesigning my classroom?
- How does my classroom space affect my students emotionally and intellectually?
- How do I make strategic choices regarding space?

CLASSROOM DESIGN

While preparing his daughter for school not too long ago, coauthor Blake found himself reflecting on his own experiences as a first grader. He remembered walking into a classroom space that was long, narrow, with white concrete walls. Coat racks were installed along the back of the room, low enough to reach, each labeled with a number. Blake's number was seventeen.

Being able to hang up his own coat was a delight. Furthermore, the pencil sharpener was attached well below the light switch and was strategically placed above a trashcan to catch the shavings. Even the chalkboard was low enough to write on and see the entire alphabet attached above in a long strip. Each of these features gave Blake a sense of power and security within this unfamiliar space. Things were going to be okay.

One drawback to his first grade experience sticks in Blake's mind—his inability to cut construction paper like his peers. He always tore the paper with each attempted cut, a common struggle for left-handed children. That is the only design flaw that Blake can recall.

Gina Childers, a science educator, recalls her first day of kindergarten at Dawson County Primary School with great clarity. Mysterious colored masking tape snaked across the floor: blue, red, yellow, green. Soon enough, she learned that each color directed students to where they should sit for different activities. Assigned colors changed for different activities and days of the week. She also learned that three specific tables were centers for STEM, art, and reading activities. The design skill that Gina's kindergarten teacher possessed helped her students know where to go and what to do.

Feeling agency, excitement, or frustration are all classroom emotions that can be heightened by *design*, a word derived from the Latin word *designare*: to designate or to choose. Design is intentional and intuitive. Instructors who care about design expend effort to deliberately plan for a specific student experience. Is that effort worth it? To kids, carefully designed spaces serve as evidence that a higher authority has taken the time to eliminate frustrations and enhance learners' agency, thereby contributing to positive life-long memories.

Applying Elementary Design Inspiration to Upper Grades Classrooms

You might expect that memories of middle and high school spaces would be equally vivid, but this is usually not the case. Too many middle and high school classrooms are unremarkable—boring, even. Of course, there are many exceptions, many of which we will describe in the following chapters. However, our experience in researching this book—studying countless elementary blogs and Pinterest boards, visiting dozens of schools over the years—has given us the impression that the majority of lower grade teachers care about design more than upper grade teachers.

Perhaps the preponderance of well-designed, lower grade classrooms is due to the fact that the biggest innovation in classroom design, Maria Montessori's introduction of child-sized classroom furniture, started in the early grades. Through testing and re-testing different classroom features, Montessori learned how children consciously and unconsciously learn new things based on playful explorations of their environment. We believe that the students of upper grades instructors who experience the big kid version of playful and organized classrooms will also benefit from these engaging environments.

Meeting Students' Needs through Design

While design helps improve a classroom's beauty and efficiency, it also enhances student motivation. We know, from Abraham Maslow's Hierarchy of Needs, that youths' motivation increases when their physiological needs, safety, social needs, self-esteem, and self-actualization needs are supported. Looking at schools through Maslow's lens, we can see how dilapidated inner city schools undermine kids' need for *safety* and beauty.[1] When classrooms fail to conscientiously support Maslow's principles, they undermine student motivation.

The purpose of classroom design and the motivation of this guide is simply this: *to enhance learning spaces, boost student performance, and positively extend the teacher's influence.* Every instance where you make well-considered changes to your classroom helps students lead self-actualized lives. Learners will feel that effort every time they step foot in your room.

DESIGN THINKING

As we have already discussed, educators can promote positive student experiences through the application of design thinking. IDEO, a company and leader in design thinking, has helped design products for 3M, Apple, Samsung, Tempur-Pedic, IKEA, and Steelcase. IDEO describes design thinking as follows:

> Bringing together what is desirable from a human point of view with what is technologically feasible and economically viable. It also allows people who aren't trained as designers to use creative tools to address a vast range of challenges.[2]

This method of integrating aesthetics and function, data and intuition, can be used by educators to address any issue facing a school (e.g., testing schedules, changes to a curriculum, the best way for students to transition between stations, and use of space). An important part of design is that it involves all stakeholders, including students.

The classroom design process involves identifying problems and understanding the context, viewing the context or problem from multiple perspectives, brainstorming solutions, redesigning the space, and observing how the solution impacts students. If the solution hasn't worked, then the process starts over again.

However, anyone who has engaged in a design protocol will tell you that the process is not orderly. In fact, the experience is represented well by

Figure 1.1   Damien Newman's design squiggle represents both uncertainty and clarity.
Source: "Damien Newman. Found here: http://cargocollective.com/central/The-Design-Squiggle. This is licensed by a Creative Commons Attribution-No Derivative Works 3.0 United States License."

Damien Newman's design squiggle,[3] as shown in Figure 1.1, where *uncertainty* is represented on the left and *clarity* on the right.

The squiggle embraces the tension between chaos and order, which really describes how human beings think and solve problems. To explore design thinking more thoroughly, we recommend two outstanding resources.

- *IDEO's Design Thinking for Educators*—IDEO's helpful workbook specifically supports K-12 education stakeholders. Download their design process toolkit (http://www.designthinkingforeducators.com).
- *Stanford's d.school*—The design school provides curated resources for those new to design thinking. Although this site is not specifically intended for educators, the protocols and resources are still applicable to classrooms (http://dschool.stanford.edu/use-our-methods/).

SETTING GOALS

Creating a vision and mission statement for your classroom (re)design will, down the road, help you make decisions. If you ever get confused during the design process, just refer back to your identified goals. Hint: the purpose will most likely relate to creating *an environment that optimizes student performance and positively extends the teacher's influence.*

Vision Statement

Organizations use vision statements to ensure that stakeholders understand the *why* of their work. Here is an inspiring vision from Special Olympics: "To transform communities by inspiring people throughout the world to open their minds, accept and include people with intellectual disabilities and thereby anyone who is perceived as different." Those bold words can change people's lives. Answering three questions will help you produce a vision statement:

- What do you see as the potential for your classroom?
- What do you hope that students experience and achieve in your space?
- What is your sky-high aspiration?

If this statement is easily understood by your learners, guardians, community stakeholders, and colleagues, it can potentially invite others to reinforce your vision. Think big! The universe rewards moxie.

Mission Statement

While the vision statement sets forth aspirational goals, the *mission statement* more concretely communicates the purpose and *how* of your work. A mission statement has three parts: (1) the value you create; (2) who you're creating it for; and (3) the expected outcome. Oprah Winfrey's personal mission statement is a good example: "To be a teacher. And to be known for inspiring my students to be more than they thought they could be."[4]

Coauthor Todd shares his personal mission statement with his classes every semester: "The purpose of teaching English is to forward social justice, suppress tyranny, and save the world!" Every year his students send him artwork with that statement because they have internalized the dream. Students who communicate your vision and mission become allies in your professional purpose.

Goals

Specific aims are called goals and describe *what* will be achieved, usually in fewer than twenty-five words.

Five characteristics of goals align with the acronym SMART:

- *Specific*—What is the goal? How do you know when it's been obtained?
- *Measurable*—How will you know when the goal is reached?
- *Acceptable*—Do stakeholders agree with what you're trying to accomplish?
- *Realistic*—Is the goal actually obtainable, given your resources?
- *Time bound*—What's the deadline?[5]

In all likelihood, your goal(s) will be associated with your students' personal and academic development.

DETERMINE THE STRENGTHS AND
WEAKNESSES OF YOUR CLASSROOM

Some teachers fall into despair when they first set eyes on their classroom. Such was the case for Bethany Kenyon, an 11th grade science teacher:

> I was given a key to my room and had to find the room myself. When I opened the door, there were desks stacked in the corner. There was stuff everywhere. I sat in the middle of the room and I stared for three hours because I had nowhere to start. It was one of the most overwhelming experiences I have ever had.

But take heart; things are never hopeless to someone with a plan and the willingness to act upon it.

As a start, write about the room without stopping for eight minutes. Note the biggest features in the space, then the smallest. Describe the walls, floor, smell, temperature, noise, shape, textures, lighting, furniture, etc. Whatever you do, focus all your attention on the physical nature of the room *without judgment*. Write about and reflect on your classroom using creative genres:

• Describe it in six words.
• Sketch it.
• Take photographs of your classroom from different student seats.
• Record measurements
• Draw an aerial view of the classroom.

At the end of one or more of these activities, you will begin to absorb the conditions of the room. Furthermore, you will begin identifying the strengths and weaknesses of the room (i.e., what needs to be minimized and what needs to be capitalized upon).

Make a list of the pros and cons of your room, as shown in Table 1.1.

EXAMINE THE SPACE FROM MULTIPLE PERSPECTIVES

A classroom doesn't just belong to the teacher. It is a public space that facilitates interactions among students, parents, fellow teachers, support staff, administrators, and visitors. Therefore, we should look at the room with their eyes. What follows are several procedures for facilitating perspective-taking.

Table 1.1 An example of a completed three-column chart that describes the pros and cons of a high school classroom.

Physical Space	Pros	Cons
Configuration	Desks are perfect for a computer lab.	The desks and chairs are aligned in a way that discourages meaningful collaboration and classroom discussion.
Technology	Every student has a computer. Both the projector and smartboard work.	Some computers work more efficiently than others. Not all students can see what is projected.
Lighting	I have large, beautiful windows in my classroom. There is adequate lighting in the room.	The sunshine creates a glare on the display, making it difficult for students to work on their assignments. The overhead lighting generates a buzzing sound.
Furniture	Desks and chairs were recently purchased.	It is difficult to arrange the classroom so students can meaningfully collaborate.
Acoustics	Sound travels well.	If students are doing collaborative group work, the noise makes it difficult for other students to concentrate.

Source: Table by Finley & Wiggs.

Empathy Activity for Perspective

Empathy maps (see Figure 1.2) can be an effective way to begin thinking about the classroom environment from a student perspective. Using chart paper, markers, and a pack of Post-it® Stickies™, record what you suspect your students are *saying*, *doing*, *thinking*, and *feeling* while in the various sections or parts your classroom.

Collect Data to Solicit Students' Perspective

Asking your students what they think and feel about their learning space can be revealing. A student in coauthor Todd's class wrote that when the instructor turned off the light to project images on the classroom screen, it made him feel "like he was in a coffin." To prevent further claustrophobia, Todd kept the lights on for the rest of the semester.

To gain more insight, ask students to complete the following prompts:

- I feel the most comfortable when . . .
- I feel the most uncomfortable when . . .

Figure 1.2   An example of an empathy map used in a school. *Source:* Image by Finley & Wiggs.

- My favorite part of the room is . . .
- My least favorite part of the room is . . .
- If I could change anything in this room, it would be . . .

Emotional Audits with Post-it® Stickies™

Asking students to emotionally *critique* your classroom can feel like inviting students to trash your design and *you*. We have found that asking students to reflect on these topics creates a culture where each learner becomes part stakeholder, part designer. One of our favorite emotional audit protocols uses Post-it® Stickies™.

Provide each student with three packs of Stickies™ (e.g., red, yellow, green). Have them identify what they like and dislike the most about the classroom by affixing a note to classroom objects (see Figures 1.3 and 1.4). Each color should represent an emotional reaction they may have to items and/or spaces within your classroom (i.e., positive, negative, and indifferent). Afterward, have your students free-write on trends and/or patterns that they noticed in the classroom. *Where are large clusters of Stickies™ posted? What do you think that means?*

Figure 1.3 In an emotional audit at Exploris Charter School, a teacher learned how much animosity students had for the classroom printer. *Source*: Sonja McKay.

The Stickies™ activity makes students' collective preferences visible and prompts discussion.

Trying out this exercise, a teacher identified how her high school students perceived the room:

> "I like having one board or area where all the important information is . . . like the agenda, calendar, due dates . . . instead of having these things all over the place."

> "I like classrooms to be colorful, but not stupid colorful. Like, I hate yellow."

> "I like when the teachers rearrange the classroom frequently. Not seating necessarily, but the way the desks are arranged. Kinda like how I change my bedroom."

After everyone has had a chance to contribute Stickies™ to the spaces and discuss findings, have your class identify the top five strengths and weaknesses of the classroom. Whatever response you receive, don't take the

Figure 1.4 During the emotional audit at Exploris Charter School, one student critiqued the speaker. [Text reads: "Aren't loud enough"]. *Source*: Sonja McKay.

comments personally. Consider the greater purpose of the activity: to create a better learning space.

Environmental Rounds

We developed an environmental rounds model based partly on patient rounds in teaching hospitals and partly on instructional rounds that are implemented by NC New Schools/Breakthrough Learning. In this activity, instructors invite their colleagues into their classrooms to think critically about problems and strengths of different rooms. The protocol involves three general stages:

- *Stage 1—Pre-Rounds*: Prior to inviting fellow teachers to visit your classroom, schedule a day and time to meet with your colleagues and share space challenges. This discussion is often no more than ten minutes, with time for colleagues to ask clarifying questions and decide how best to collect classroom data.

- *Stage 2—Rounds*: During this phase, colleagues visit your classroom and make notes about your design challenges. These rounds may occur during a class or when students are out of the room. The format of your colleagues' notes may depend on the type of questions you asked during *stage 1*.
- *Stage 3—Post-Rounds*: After re-stating your question, colleagues share notes from their rounds while you silently record the information. Keep in mind that this part of the process is formal and should be tightly managed by a volunteer facilitator to ensure that everyone has the same opportunity to contribute ideas. The facilitator should also interrupt feedback that takes on an evaluative tone.

IDENTIFYING THEME AND PRIORITIZING SOLUTIONS

After completing any of the emotional audits, environmental rounds, student surveys, or empathy maps, make generalizations about the classroom problems. Some teachers may create *affinity diagrams*, where they write one thing on a notecard and begin reorganizing these notes into categories.[6] From those categories, themes will organically emerge.

Once you have identified the major themes and/or challenges facing your classroom, brainstorm solutions. *What things can be done to enhance the positives and minimize the negatives that you, students, and colleagues identified?*

One exercise we like is called *stepladder brainstorming*. A problem statement is articulated to a group of people. For example: "Students in back can't see the entire whiteboard." Participants are then given time to write solutions on paper. Then in groups of two, brainstormers share their best ideas. Next, three-person teams are formed, where the new member shares his/her ideas before the other two continue their thoughts; this surfaces diverse perspectives. Stepladder brainstorming continues until the entire group has shared their ideas.[7] Afterward, have the group look at the list to see if any of the ideas are feasible. You'll be surprised at how quickly the brainstorming process produces actionable ideas.

CREATE AND IMPLEMENT ACTION PLAN

After brainstorming, it's time to make an action plan—a list of steps that need to be taken in order to achieve specific goals. Action plans often involve:

1. Resource identification, such as . . .
   - Students' parents or community volunteers
   - Businesses or nonprofits

- PTAs or university partnerships
- Money-generating events
- Crowdfunding (e.g., GoFundMe, Kickstarter, and Indiegogo)
- Education grants
2. Timeline of action items
   - What happens first, next, etc.?
   - Who is responsible for which items?
3. Processes for keeping stakeholders informed of the process
   - Send out regular updates
   - Report on progress at meetings
4. Concrete outcomes
   - What are the deliverables?
   - How do you know when the job is done?
5. Opportunities to celebrate accomplishments

FINAL THOUGHTS

As you execute the design process, it is natural to feel overwhelmed with the amount of choices available to you. But keep positive, keep an open mind, and take small steps. And when obstacles occur, consult your brainstorming partners. You will be surprised at the dramatic results.

Find more resources, images, and links related to this chapter at http://www. todd-finley.com/classroom-design-chapter-1-classroom-design-process/.

NOTES

1. Maslow, A. (1968). *Toward a Psychology of Being* (2nd ed.). New York: Van Nostrand.

2. Kelly, David M. (2002). About IDEO | IDEO. Retrieved June 11, 2015, from http://www.ideo.com/about/.

3. Newman, D. (n.d.). The Design Squiggle—Central. Retrieved June 21, 2015.

4. Vozza, S. (2014, February 25). Personal Mission Statements of 5 Famous CEOs (And Why You Should Write One Too). Retrieved June 21, 2015.

5. Power, D. (n.d.). What Are Characteristics of a Good Goal Statement? PlanningSkills.com. Retrieved June 22, 2015.

6. Jiro, K. (n.d.). Affinity Diagrams: Organizing Information and Ideas into Common Themes. Retrieved June 22, 2015.

7. Rogelberg, S., Barnes-Farrell, J., & Lowe, C. (1992). The Stepladder Technique. Retrieved June 22, 2015.

Chapter 2

The Basic Parts of a Room

Look at your learning space with 21st-century eyes: Does it work for what we know about learning today, or just for what we knew about learning in the past?

—*The Third Teacher*

Guiding Questions

- What are elements of the classroom space that people don't often consider?
- How can you use tools to make design decisions easier?
- How do you contrast *design* and *decoration*?

HOW TO THINK ABOUT DESIGN

Being a student-centered or teacher-centered instructor is often revealed in your classroom design. Do you use the empty space by the chalkboard as your stage? Are you the focal point? Perhaps your space is more accommodating to a variety of student-centered activities? Regardless of its arrangement, your room should *inspire and challenge students to be their best selves.*

But how? There is no "best" design because all instructors have to negotiate different factors: budgets, room size, types of technologies, and access to previously used furniture. Additionally, some classrooms are conventionally rectangular, whereas some have oddball shapes. And who could have imagined the popularity of balance ball chairs?

The decisions you make, whatever they are, should ideally proceed from three types of thinking:

- *Macro thinking* is taking a big picture view, visualizing long-term goals, and prioritizing the finished result. This approach works best when you're relaxed and reflecting outside of the classroom, not when you are running up against a deadline.
- *Micro thinking* involves identifying specific daily details to accomplish in order to move toward your big picture goal. This type of thinking is useful when you are in the classroom, solving specific problems.
- *Intuition* is your inner voice that tells you what will and won't work. Be still, breathe deeply, and reflect in order to fully tap into your intuition. As you imagine different solutions, does your body tense up or do you feel energized? That's your gut helping you make decisions.

As you read about the different parts of the classroom described in the following sections, stay open to different options. And use all three decision-making orientations: macro thinking, micro thinking, and intuition.

HOW IMPORTANT IS THOUGHTFUL ROOM DESIGN?

Have you ever entered a building or room for the first time and felt enhanced—felt your body relax and spirit elevate? People lucky enough to visit places like Abu Camp in Botswana; Pixar Headquarters in Emeryville, California; or Stadium High School, which overlooks the Puget Sound, are quite likely to notice a change in their breathing patterns. They may feel elated when they realize that the creators of these facilities understood their minds and hearts, and cared enough to physically support both.

The effect of human-made environments on people's brains is not subjective. According to research studies, we all have measurable responses to the design of a space. For example:

- *Air quality*—In 2011, Kenn Fisher, head of the OECD Programme on Educational Building, stated that air quality, temperature, and lighting is linked to student behaviors and academic performance.[1]
- *Updating schools*—Student achievement scores were shown to improve by 5 percent when building conditions were modernized, according to another study.[2]
- *Setting and friendships*—In the 1940s, sociologist Kurt Back, along with psychologists Leon Festinger and Stanley Schachter, found that physical space could demonstrably foster friendship development by encouraging people to cross into others' spaces.
- *Comfort and academics*—Discussing a study of twenty-five first graders, Dr. Sheryl Reinisch, director of the Early Childhood Education Programs at Concordia University, said that comfortable rooms help students learn.[3]

To be clear, design's impact on the brain does not fall into the pseudo-science category of, say, the power of a hyacinth to build self-esteem. Research on constructed environments in general and classrooms in particular have occurred for decades.

Design vs. Decoration

A quick clarification is in order before this chapter addresses common room elements. *Interior design* should not be confused with *decoration*. Interior design is the art and science of understanding people's behavior in order to create functional spaces for them. Decoration is the furnishing or adorning of a space with fashionable or beautiful things.[4]

In some cases, careful decoration can undermine design. This phenomenon was present when we visited an elementary school teacher's classroom that was decorated from floor to ceiling with zebra print. Besides making the room feel crowded and oppressive, the decoration failed to consider how the aesthetics overwhelmed her students. Boys, in particular, were alienated by the aggressive frilly quality of the room. In a post–Caitlyn Jenner world where Facebook now lists fifty-six possible gender choices for members' personal profiles, instructors should stay alert to the fact that our values are often communicated by how we decorate and who our posters celebrate.

START WITH A CLASSROOM FLOOR PLANNER

A quick way to coordinate how all the elements of your classroom can support your favorite activities is to draw a floor plan. Paper and pencil will work fine, but free online tools like Classroom Architect (http://classroom.4teachers.org/) provide helpful grids that can be resized based on your space's specific dimensions and tools that allow users to drag premade objects into different arrangements. Does the beanbag chair fit by the window or is it better tucked behind the mini fridge? What's better, the kidney or round shaped table? Use the floor planner to playfully consider where you might position the following objects that are discussed in the sections that follow.

MAJOR CLASSROOM COMPONENTS

In the following paragraphs, we will provide some highlights of physical components that are common to most classrooms—discussing some elements within your control that you may not have considered. For example, what is the best air temperature for learning? Read on to find out.

Tables

To state the obvious, tables should support the tasks that are most important to the grade and content that you teach. For example, tables are the preferred choice of science labs, shops, and art instructors because they accommodate multiple materials. If possible, choose tables that raise or lower, allowing students to make adjustments that support their size and working preference.

Ideally, there should be about ten inches of space between the top of a seat or stool and the bottom of the table. Rectangular tables can be moved to support cooperative learning groups or shifted into a big U-shape for whole class discussion.

Tables come with features that accommodate various content-specific activities. Art teachers appreciate tables with stain-resistant laminate. Computer instructors prefer height-adjustable computer tables that are narrow and long for placement against a wall, thereby minimizing the classroom footprint and allowing the teacher visual access to students' monitors. Science teachers prefer lab tables with a chemical guard, plastic laminate, or epoxy resin top and that feature storage.

Support students with special needs by providing wheelchair accessible tables that are knob adjustable or of the horseshoe wheelchair activity table variety as required under Title III. These come in different sizes and prices, from $300 up to $3,000. Finally, regulations require that placement of the tables, just like the placement of seating, adheres to fire and safety guidelines.

Seating

Seat and desk combinations come in all varieties: open front, lift lid, tablet arm, multistudent, extra large, triangle (which makes collaboration easier), with or without a wire basket, sit and stand, study carrels, light and heavy, etc. When looking for pupil stations, key features beyond affordability include *durability* (Is it made of welded steel or high-pressure laminate fiberboard? Is it scratch resistant?) and *comfort* (Is the size right? Does it have ergonomic contours? Is the back vented?). Even expensive chair-desk combinations can cause great discomfort to overweight students who, out of shame, are unlikely to complain.

Since pupil stations take up so much space, it is useful to consider them in the context of the entire classroom and productive classroom activities such as individual work, partner pairing, small group work, and Socratic seminar circles.

Seating Configuration Apps

Three apps can help you brainstorm some general seating arrangements:

- *Smart Seat*, by Cornwall ($4.99), allows you choose the number of rows and seats for those rows, then import student names and faces by either dragging learners onto specific seats or selecting "scramble" for a randomized selection. *For iOS devices.*
- *Be Seated*, by Jellyfish Pi, allows you to create a visual class roster with names, photos, and desks arranged as you like, with or without a grid. Randomize seat assignments are also available. *For iOS devices.*
- *Safety Attendance*, by For Safety Solutions, lets you arrange students desks. The app offers multiple features: attendance, roll call, and note-tracker among others. *For Android devices.*

A comprehensive discussion of how to configure seating to support your favorite classroom activities is featured in chapter 4.

Supplies

The number of supply areas throughout your classroom will depend on what grade and content you teach, as well as how many supplies you store in your room. Make sure the supplies are well organized, labeled, and—if safety is not an issue—at a height appropriate for your students. Because they can monitor supply levels easily, many teachers like crates or translucent tubs, which can be purchased at supply or major retail stores.

Walls

Classroom walls are important instructional real estate. That's why walls should aesthetically feature important classroom information: standards, rules, schedules, posters, student work, awards, a duty roster, a timeline, goals, and objectives, to name a few.

We're often asked how to get posters and signs to stick to cinder block by teachers who are tired of finding posted materials on the floor every morning. We've found that a hot glue gun will attach almost anything to the classroom wall, as long as the material is not too heavy. Here is one trick to enable quick mounting of signs and posters: use a hot glue gun to affix velcro to the walls, then simply place velcro on the new poster. Stikki-Clips® also work well with cinder block and are reusable. Their strong white plastic clips and dependable Stikki-Wax backs cling to most surfaces.

We all have a favorite wall color, but how does color affect the brain? According to color psychologist Angela Wright, "The different wavelengths strike the eye in different ways. In the retina, they are converted into electrical impulses that pass to the part of the brain known as the hypothalamus, which governs our endocrine system and hormones, *and much of our activity.*"[5]

Wright says that yellow makes you optimistic, while blue is associated with productivity. However, she likes to add some orange "to introduce a bit of balance, a bit of emotion." The intensity of a color is also important. Low saturation colors (like the color of butter) are more soothing, while high saturation colors (like a lemon) activate the brain.

Edward Deming, the famous management consultant, encouraged institutions not to post slogans or exhortations on the walls—believing that these messages did not contribute to productivity. An exception would be motivational posters that students develop and design on their own. Some teachers ask students to lend their favorite posters to the classroom for the year as a way for young learners to see that the classroom reflects their interests.

Create the illusion of more space by hanging mirrors in your room. For windowless classrooms, create the illusion of a window by hanging curtains around a mirror. Don't hang a mirror at the front of the room, otherwise students will be checking themselves out instead of focusing on you.

Storage

Storage solutions are abundant on the web and in major retail stores. One of our favorite solutions is a mobile Sterilite™ storage cart with four see-through drawers that can hold books or teaching materials. DIY containers made from old ice-milk buckets, detergent bottles (for paint brushes), and decorated cereal boxes or shoe containers are green ways to get organized. Writes one anonymous instructor on Stretcher.com, "Hang a decorative shower curtain between a wall and a large art cabinet if you have one and store all kinds of things behind it! I go from floor to the top of the curtain with items in boxes that are labeled with the contents."[6]

Shelves

For classroom libraries, textbook sets, or a place to store your professional development binders, shelves are inexpensive and convenient. Many teachers paint wooden crates, then they bind them with the opening faced out toward the classroom. If you use more than three, attach them to each other and the wall for safety using screws and a drill. Resting a board on two file boxes is a quick way to create display space and file storage. Another key to organized shelves is to keep items labeled in logical containers, with binders for papers and tubs for small objects.

Teacher's Area

The teacher's desk area is a sanctuary and place for essential materials. Place only essential materials on your desk. Even a few trinkets add clutter.

Chapter 7 will describe how to organize your desk. But for now, just remember that everything—*everything*—on your desk should have a designated home, so that no time is wasted searching for items. We also recommend that you use a label maker to affix messages to your supplies so that borrowed items are returned.

Empty Spaces

Resist the urge to fill a classroom with desks, furniture, and materials. Remember, when they arrive, thirty student bodies will take up a lot of space. They need elbow room.

The following questions are based, in part, on prompts developed by Marlynn Clayton and Mary Forton's *Classroom Spaces That Work* to help teachers think about how they are using space:

- Is there enough room in the meeting/mini-lesson space for students to sit comfortably with their classmates?
- Is there enough room for lining up at the door for a fire drill or dismissal with approximately ten inches of space between each child?
- Do the aisles allow kids to travel without bumping seated peers? Can students pass each other in the aisle?
- Are the spaces around desks wide enough to allow the instructor to conference with students from a stool with castors?
- Do you have a time-out space for students who are disruptive?[7]

MAKING THE ORDINARY CLASSROOM EXTRAORDINARY

Pinterest and The Cornerstone for Teachers[8] are two sources of inspiration for making your room inviting. Three ideas we like:

- Use beach blankets as floor rugs. When they get dirty, simply throw them in the wash.
- Potted trees with white LED lights look festive all year round.
- Laminate student-made posters on academic topics. By the way, every poster looks better with a border.
  Use patio furniture in your reading area. It's durable and easy to clean.

Indoor/Outdoor Garden

Your horticulture experiments can continue during winter with grow lights or a room with plenty of natural light. Place your seed container (with drainage holes) on a large tray to avoid water damage, then grow root vegetables or fruit crops. Garden shops will advise you on what soil and seeds will garner the best result.

Class Pets

Kids love greeting a classroom pet every day. But think through what type of pet is safe, what enclosure is appropriate, what chemicals will be needed to clean the pet habitat, what pet handling rules will need to be posted, and what care arrangements will be made on holidays. Three resources for learning more about proper pet care in the classroom include:

- The Humane Society
- Centers for Disease Control and Prevention
- United States Department of Agriculture—Animal Care Program

CRITICAL INSTRUCTIONAL COMPONENTS

Chalkboard or Whiteboard?

According to the American Academy of Allergy, Asthma, and Immunology, chalk dust is one of the triggers of asthma and allergy attacks. Meanwhile, dark text on a light background allows for faster processing of information and comprehension.[9] For these reasons, go with a whiteboard, if you have a choice.

If you're stuck with a blackboard, there is a way you can help reduce chalk dust. Marilyn Redmond, a second grade teacher in Ontario, Canada, recommends the following:

> I take a clean small towel and put a little bit of lemon oil on it. I place the towel in a Ziploc® bag and leave it overnight so that the lemon oil soaks into the towel. After I erase the blackboard, I clean it with the towel and it removes all the chalk dust without leaving any streaks.[10]

Popular Classroom Technologies (Not Software)

More classrooms are taking advantage of the twenty-first-century tech boom. Here are some commonly recommended classroom technologies:

- *Smart TV*—like a regular TV, but they connect to the Internet.
- *LCD Projector*—projects computer images, video, data, etc. on a screen or flat white surface.

- *Interactive Whiteboard (Smart Board)*—a touch-sensitive digital whiteboard connected to a computer that can store information written on it. The interactive whiteboard has its own compatible software.
- *CD Player (or computer with speakers)*
- *Audience Response Systems (Clickers)*—instantly and formatively assess student knowledge, save information, and even grade answers.
- *Document Camera (Doc Cam)*—a real-time image capture device for displaying written work or an object to an audience.
- *Notebook, Chromebook, desktop, and tablet computers*—keep getting less expensive and more powerful.

Reading Zone and Class Library

If you want to promote literacy, create a cozy space that invites students to relax and focus on a good book. To make this type of space optimal, provide comfortable seating, lamp light, carpet, and sound dampeners. Erin Klein, a second grade Michigan instructor, outfits her reading zone with "rocking chairs, benches, and patio chairs, and in the back corner of the room, a breakfast nook is nestled beside a floor lamp and a large artificial tree."[11] This oasis communicates that it pays to be a reader. Also, even struggling readers become interested in books when they are displayed on a tiered rack or spindle.

THINGS YOU NOTICE WHEN THEY AREN'T RIGHT

Noise

Noise becomes distracting for students when they can't control the sound. A printer beeping, a door slamming, hallway laughter, or desks scraping against the floor can all reduce reading comprehension and general productivity. As noise levels rise, the brain works less efficiently. Executive functions like planning and reasoning become disrupted. Moderate ambient noise, meanwhile, has been shown by a 2012 study to enhance creativity.[12]

Ask your administrator to buy Roxul Rockboard 80, Mineral Wool Board, or other inexpensive acoustic insulation. If a parent or administrator asks why, explain that noise can release excess cortisol, which impairs the prefrontal cortex's ability to store short-term memories.

Light

In the 1940s, energy-efficient fluorescent lighting was mass-produced and installed in classrooms everywhere. Since then, the controversy over whether and to what degree fluorescent lighting affects cognition has not been resolved. Meanwhile, exposure to dim lighting or artificial lighting over a period of several days reduces a person's cortisol levels significantly (making their energy levels less stable and increasing stress), according to a 2012 study. It also makes people sleepier.

Temperature

Class temperature above 77 degrees Fahrenheit negatively impacts mental output and attention spans.[13] Another study of office productivity by researchers at Cornell University demonstrated that raising the temperature from 68 degrees to 73 degrees Fahrenheit reduced keyboarding errors by 44 percent among adult office workers and increases output by 150 percent.[14] The logic of this is as follows: when it's cold, people become uncomfortable and distracted. So keep classroom temperatures in the sweet spot of 74–76 degrees Fahrenheit.

Do you know why the interiors of commercial airplanes are so cold? It's because the flight attendants get hot pushing heavy food carts up and down the aisles—and they keep asking the pilot to lower the heat. Like flight attendants, teachers may move around the classroom significantly more than their students. Be careful, the room might be colder than you think. Also, because the classroom is composed of different micro-environments, the temperature by the vent may be several degrees warmer than by the window. Furthermore, excessive humidity can adversely affect psychological function.[15]

CONTENT AREA CONSIDERATIONS

Laying out all the classroom features that every content area should possess is beyond the scope of this guide. However, we would like to emphasize the importance of authenticity. When students walk into a classroom lab outfitted with safety stations, lab stools, lab carts, gooseneck faucets, nestable fireproof storage trays, gas fittings, and a teacher's laminated demonstration desk affixed with an overhead mirror, their brains are cued to think like scientists. Does your journalism room look like a newsroom? Does your art classroom look like a studio? Creating environments that imitate the authentic conditions of the real world help establish a disciplinary mind-set.

EIGHT SOLUTIONS FOR WORKING WITH TINY CLASSROOMS

Lack of space is the most common complaint that we hear about classrooms. Meanwhile, budget cuts across the country have resulted in overcrowding.

The good news is that there are some simple solutions to creating more space. Here's the bad news: you might not be able to keep all your classroom materials and furniture in your room.

So, how do you make your tiny classroom into a better environment for learning?

1. *Get rid of objects that are rarely used.* If the object hasn't been used for two to three years, trash it, or give it away. Objects that are used only occasionally, like that full-sized easel, can be stored down the hall in the supply closet.
2. *Keep objects that serve multiple functions.* Besides holding a projector, a media cart might also be the place where you store the annotated instructor texts and handouts for the day; so that's a keeper—but only if you regularly project images. Bonus tip: use velcro to attach a skirt to the cart to conceal clutter.
3. *Give away over-sized furniture, the biggest space hogs.* Recycle that oak table if its footprint is too large.
4. *Junk anything that is purely aesthetic.* That plastic tree decorated with hanging origami cranes might be a favorite object, but because it doesn't have an obvious learning utility, it's got to go.
5. *Take advantage of free space.* Buy cheap bins to store materials, then place them underneath tables. When possible, buy table skirts to hide the bins. A twelve-foot-long plastic skirt can be purchased for about five dollars.
6. *Prioritize students' needs.* Since there are far more students in the room than teachers, instructor materials should occupy only a fraction of the space.
7. *Get "extras" out of the room.* Don't keep extra seats in the room, or two half-filled bookcases when one will do.
8. *Partition space.* Room dividers now feature tackable acoustical fabric that dampens the noise in tiny rooms—a useful feature when activity centers are in progress. Use a mobile whiteboard to section off areas of the classroom for small group work, peer feedback, or tutoring. Expandable walls now provide flex space.

Nancy Paulson, an elementary teacher, adapted her super-tiny room into a learning space by providing only fourteen desks for all twenty-six students! Paulson placed tables, chairs, rugs, and furniture in the corners of the room, not just the middle. Then, Paulson took careful note during the next couple of weeks of what spaces students gravitated toward and then expanded on those sections.[16]

WHAT ABOUT TINY BUDGETS?

Even with a small budget, teachers are able to pick up couches at yard sales, ask parent carpenters to build cabinets and bookcases, and buy dirt cheap storage bins at The Dollar Store. Classrooms by Walmart (http://www.walmart.com/classrooms/) have a classroom website with a registry to share with parents. Or, you can post needed materials on a crowd funding platform like Donors Choose or Adopt-A-Classroom. Freecycle (https://www.freecycle.org/) is a worldwide community that gives old items away. Finally, browse through the free section of the Craigslist page for your area.

FINAL THOUGHTS

Thinking about all the elements needed to create a successful learning space can feel daunting. To help you review important considerations when you are making classroom choices, we created the mnemonic **F-CABIN** checklist for you, which stands for *flexibility, concentration, attention, belonging, interaction, neatness.*

- *Flexibility*—Can the students and instructor(s) easily transition to functional spaces (such as a class library, literacy center, computer area, stage, and reading nook)? Do the transition areas create potential bottlenecks?
- *Concentration*—What features of the room could be enhanced or minimized to help students focus? Are sound-absorbing materials needed to defuse noise from either the inside or outside of the classroom? Are the areas where students are active—such as the conference table—as far away as possible from the silent work-study carrels? Is there enough natural and artificial light for students to view books, chalkboards, and bulletin boards? Do all the student seats allow for an unobstructed view of the whiteboard, chalkboard, and screen-projected information?
- *Attention*—Show off valued materials. Is the fire extinguisher well marked? Elementary school teacher Chris Weaver displays books by inserting them into inexpensive vinyl rain gutters attached to her walls.
- *Belonging*—Learners should feel like the space is theirs. Put up pictures of kids and exemplary work. Put up posters that feature diverse faces.
- *Interaction*—By turning their seats, can learners quickly work with a small group of peers? Are there wide aisles that allow students to retrieve commonly used materials like textbooks, notebook computers, journals, and art supplies? Can the instructor easily reach and interact with any student?
- *Neatness*—Are supplies, tools, furniture, and books stored away? Two valuable resources for beating classroom clutter are *Scholastic's Survival Guide* and *Pinterest's DIY Classroom*.

Find more resources, images, and links related to this chapter at http://www. todd-finley.com/design-chapter-2-the-basic-parts-of-the-room/.

NOTES

1. Crump, K. (n.d.). Building Better Outcomes: The Impact of School Infrastructure on Student Outcomes and Behaviour. Retrieved June 22, 2015.

2. Edwards, M. (1992). Building Condition, Parental Involvement and Student Achievement in the D.C. Public School System. M.Ed. Dissertation. Washington, DC, Georgetown University.

3. How Comfortable Classrooms Lead to a Better Student Community. (2012, October 19). Retrieved June 22, 2015.

4. Designer v. Decorator. (n.d.). Retrieved June 22, 2015, from http://www. modspacedesign.com/mod-space-home/design-resources/the-difference-between-an-interior-designer-and-an-interior-decorator/.

5. Bailey, C. (2013, June 27). The exact color to paint your office to become the most productive. Retrieved June 22, 2015.

6. Classroom Storage Ideas. (2002, August 2). Retrieved June 22, 2015, from http://www.stretcher.com/stories/02/02aug19a.cfm.

7. Clayton, M., & Forton, M. (2001). *Classroom Spaces That Work*. Greenfield, MA: Northeast Foundation for Children.

8. Watson, A. (2003, July 1). Creating a Cozy Classroom, The Cornerstone. Retrieved June 22, 2015.

9. Is a Chalkboard the Right Choice? (2012). Retrieved June 22, 2015, from http://stonehousesigns.com/news/is-a-chalkboard-the-right-choice.

10. Redmond, M. (n.d.). Teacher Resources and Classroom Management: Clean Blackboards & Chalkboards. Retrieved June 23, 2015.

11. Klein, E. (2013, August 1). Designing Your Classroom Space (With Before and After Photos). Retrieved June 23, 2015.

12. Mehta, R., Zhu, R. J., & Cheema, A. (2012). Is Noise Always Bad? Exploring the Effects of Ambient Noise on Creative Cognition. *Journal of Consumer Research,* 39(4), 784–799.

13. McCardle, R. (1966). *Thermal Environment and Learning*. Columbia, MO: University of Missouri.

14. Hedge, A. (Director) (2004, June 1). Linking Environmental Conditions to Productivity. Eastern Ergonomics Conference and Exposition. Lecture conducted from Ithaca, NY.

15. Sharma, V., Pichan, G., & Panwar, M. (1983). Differential effects of hot-humid and hot-dry environments on mental functions. *International Archives of Occupational and Environmental Health International*, 4(52), 315–327. Retrieved June 23, 2015.

16. Boushey, G., & Moser, J. (2012). Design Help for Small Classrooms. Retrieved June 23, 2015.

Chapter 3

The Second Teacher
Bulletin Boards

A bulletin board can be both educational and decorative.

—Michael Gravois

Guiding Questions

- What is the science behind designing bulletin boards that support learning?
- How do you create bulletin boards that draw students' attention?
- How do you make bulletin boards interactive?

DON'T JUST DECORATE, EDUCATE!

Facing demands to meet national and state standards, teachers cannot afford to merely decorate their bulletin boards (BBs). They need to view their boards as an important instructional tool that enhances the academic focus of the classroom. This is not an easy task. Consider all the important functions of a BB:

- displaying standards-based content
- inspiring students
- reinforcing concepts, skills, rules, and routines
- showcasing exemplary student work, photos, and awards
- inviting student interaction
- reinforcing community
- using alliterative, playful, and memorable titles
- adhering to visual communication principles

While not all successful BBs are aligned with the aforementioned principles, they have a better chance of enhancing content understanding and improving class functioning when those elements are considered. Furthermore, effective BBs are always "on duty"—displaying content to the class at all times. That's why we call bulletin boards *the second teacher.*

INVITE STUDENTS TO BE DISPLAY COLLABORATORS

While teacher-made bulletin boards dominate most classrooms, instructors don't need to create them alone. In fact, investment in the class culture and curriculum can be enhanced by challenging students to collaboratively design a display that visually organizes their content understanding.[1]

The Early Childhood Environment Rating Scale gives a high rating to displays "that feature work in which children select the media or the subject and create a personal response rather than a formula response."[2] When working with student-produced work, take care to avoid posting misconceptions or misspellings.

Consider creating a graphic organizer on a bulletin board in front of students while introducing a new concept. Seventh and eighth grade English teacher Barbara Colvin has "students 'draw pictures' of adverbs. She posts the pictures and refers to them during adverb lessons. The student-created visuals are especially simple and effective."

Also, English teachers can create a BB that displays the five stages of the writing process: *prewriting, drafting, revising, editing,* and *publishing.* As the board grows more elaborate, perhaps by describing different strategies for each stage (see Figure 3.1), students' conceptual knowledge deepens. Later, instructors can refer students back to the display to review the content when the need arises.

Stages of the Writing Process

1. **prewriting**: freewriting, mind-mapping, listing points to cover
2. **drafting**: meta-writing (describing what needs to happen in the essay)
3. **revising**: cut the paper into separate paragraphs and re-arrange
4. **editing**: point at each word while reading aloud, remove passive verbs (if possible)
5. **publishing**: post your work on a blog or discussion forum

---

Figure 3.1   An example of a bulletin board that supports English language arts conceptual knowledge by listing strategies aligned with the five stages of the writing process.
Source: Chart by Finley & Wiggs.

Writes Pernille Ripp about her seventh grade English bulletin board, "As always, I am showcasing covers of what I read (students will be doing the same inside the room later in the year); but this year I am also showing what I am writing and why."[3]

INFORMATION BOARDS

Information bulletin boards offer another channel of communication that supports a smooth-functioning classroom. Examples of information bulletin boards:

- Classroom rules
- Goals
- Curriculum calendar
- Emergency procedures
- Weekly objectives
- Things students can do when they finish an assignment early:
    i. Read a preselected book
    ii. Study your vocabulary words
    iii. Answer a journal prompt
    iv. Do extension worksheets
    v. Write a book review
    vi. Write down your addition facts
    vii. Do a math game on a classroom iPad
    viii. Compose a letter to the teacher about what you are struggling with
    ix. Read and respond to an article suggested by "The Learning Network" section of the online *New York Times*.
- Classroom chores
- Classroom data in the form of an assignment thermometer or printed Excel Spreadsheet graph (keeping individual student information private)
- The school bell schedule

Bulletin boards can be small or big, permanent or portable. They can be placed in unorthodox locations, such as the front of the teacher's desk or cabinet, and above the room door or chalkboard. If teachers do not have a bulletin board (or the budget for one), they can craft one by covering substantial cardboard with wrapping paper and hanging the makeshift BB from the ceiling.

BBs can also promote social-emotional learning. Carol Miller, a middle school counselor in New York, asks her Lansing Middle School students to name one thing that they could do to make the school a better place.

After completing the project, students receive jelly bracelets with the saying, *"What you do matters!"* and are treated to pies donated by local businesses.[4]

GENERAL DO'S AND DON'TS

Do

- Feature essential academic content or dispositions that will lead to higher academic performances
- Make sure the board has an identifiable purpose
- Feature students' contributions
- Create BBs that invite students to interact (e.g., asking questions that can be answered by considering different artifacts displayed)
- Make your BBs invite curiosity
- Keep them uncluttered
- Position them in well-lighted parts of the room at a height that is age-appropriate
- Time new BBs with the launch of new units
- Use "plasticized paper" to avoid premature fading
- Allow all students an opportunity to see their work displayed
- Use sticky Velcro to affix heavier materials
- Be creative in considering where to locate bulletin boards (e.g., the front of the teacher's desk)

Don't

- Slap up a commercialized bulletin board
- Post cartoon images of kids that trivialize children
- Display stereotyped activities (e.g., Chinese children flying dragon kites at a parade or girls cooking)
- Let the design elements, like the border or background, overpower students' artistic contributions
- Forget to make a rough sketch before creating your BB
- Make your board too busy
- Avoid spray mount (some children's asthma might be activated)
- Post completed worksheets
- Feature decorations that privilege a specific religious holiday
- Allow misspellings or inaccurate information to be displayed
- Use purple or blue (these colors fade quickly in sunlight)
- Believe that all BBs must stay "within the borders"

BEFORE YOU BEGIN

Before creating your bulletin boards, take this shopping list to a nearby crafts store so you'll have all your needed BB supplies:

- Chalk line kit (for straight lines)
- Scissors
- Ruler
- Glue
- Good stapler and Draper heavy duty staple remover (tip: Staple at a diagonal on harder BB surfaces to allow the staples to be easily removed.)[5]
- Velcro sticky strips
- Push pins and thumbtacks
- Stencils
- Masking and clear tape
- Markers

DESIGN BASICS

The Border

To enhance eyeball appeal, *Kim's Korner* suggests making bulletin board borders with wide ribbons, hot-glued crayons, or laminated wrapping paper cut into strips. Another option is to use nontraditional Christmas tree tinsel for an eye-catching border. You can always visit the "borders and trim" section of Staples, or buy silver cupcake holders or Hawaiian leis at a dollar store to create tactile borders.[6]

Space

The arrangement should not be too complex. Allow plenty of blank space. Using the rule of thirds, "do not place the subject at the center, or prevent a horizon from appearing to divide the picture in half."[7]

Colors

Be cognizant of the seasons: yellow, red, brown, and orange in spring; black, powder-blue, white, and red for winter; orange, red, pink, and gold for fall. Or search Interest for other "seasonal colors."

Typography

Keep to two typefaces per board, but use interesting combinations: serif and sans serif, heavy-weighted lines with thin lines; one big typeface and one small.

Images

Avoid apples, clip art, and cheesy stock photography of people. Particularly at the secondary level, students perceive these artifacts as patronizing—not reflecting the sophistication and complexity of the contemporary adolescent. Make sure printed images are not pixelated and that they match the color scheme of the background.

EXAMPLES OF BOARD TOPICS

The theme or topic of your board should be obvious to students and easily read from across the classroom. Keep your title under eight words. However, you can put something on the board that challenges students to think, such as questions about famous women inventors. Here are more topic ideas:

- Vocabulary words, definitions, and translations in Spanish
- Have parents write encouraging statements during open house. Post them under a board heading that says "YOU CAN DO IT!"
- "Where Will You Go to College?" Pin flags with student names on chosen universities and colleges.
- "Got Fitness?"—Illustrate multiple ways to get fit.
- "Ensemble Groups"—Illustrate and define duets, trios, sextets, and octets.
- "Pizza Fractions"—Have students represent different fractions with pizzas illustrated on tag board.
- Plant or animal taxonomy
- Author of the week with QR codes linked to specific books
- Story starters
- Test-taking tips
- Word wall
- Bell ringers described for each day of the week
- "Question of the Week"—By Thursday, each student posts his or her answers.
- Cereal box literature projects:
  On one side, students list the nutritional facts of the plot.
  On the other side, students define important vocabulary in the text.
  On the top, kids list and describe the main characters.
  On the bottom, students write their name, title of the book, and the name of the author.
  On the front, students write a literary cereal title, like "Sour Grape Cereal (*The Grapes of Wrath*)." Then, they compose a slogan about the theme and illustrate the theme of the text.[8]
- "Mighty Math Story Problems"—This BB can include tag board with student-created story problems, answers, and explanations on the back.
- Twister Game Sheet with math numerals to add, subtract, or multiply

The more interactive you can make the bulletin board, the better. For example, a math teacher's fourth grade bulletin board has laminated problem elements that can be switched out on a weekly basis and invite students to interact. "This can be a math warm up or can be used as a station or on a menu during math workshop. [Also, it can] either enrich my current unit or review a previously taught concept."[9]

Bulletin boards add another channel for communicating difficult curriculum, deepening students' conceptual understanding, making connections between the content and the real world, inspiring further investigation, and building the classroom community. In addition, BBs make a powerful statement about what a teacher values most, so make them count!

RESOURCES

Places to Purchase Bulletin Board Supplies

Don't hesitate to ask parents for materials or find BB supplies at yard sales. However, there are many options for buying commercial bulletin board materials, as evidenced by the list below. To save money, coordinate with colleagues in order to purchase items in bulk.

FINAL THOUGHTS

A growing faction of the education community insists that the bulletin board should *exclusively* contain strategies, processes, guidelines, content knowledge, cues, and items that support skill development. However, totally removing whimsy from your bulletin board would bleach out the most colorful and rewarding part of teaching and learning: enchantment. And nobody wants that.

Find more resources, images, and links related to this chapter at http://www. todd-finley.com/classroom-design-chapter-3-the-2nd-teacher-bulletin-boards/.

NOTES

1. Steele, K. (2007, November 14). Bulletin Board Borders. Retrieved September 20, 2015, from http://www.kimskorner4teachertalk.com/classmanagement/bb/borders.htm.

2. Tarr, P. (2004, May 1). "Consider the Walls." National Association for the Education of Young Children, pp. 1–5. Retrieved January 3, 2016, from http://www.naeyc.org/files/yc/file/200405/ConsidertheWalls.pdf.

3. Ripp, P. (2014, August 29). "Classroom Tour 2014." Blogging through the Fourth Dimension. Retrieved January 3, 2016, from http://pernillesripp. com/2014/08/29/classroom-tour-2014/.

4. Miller, C. (2013). "What You Do Matters at Mix It Up Day." The Middle School Counselor. Retrieved September 28, 2014, from http://www.themiddleschoolcounselor.com/2013/02/what-you-do-matters-at-mix-it-up-day.html.

5. Hartley, L. (2014). "A Display Makers Toolbox." Classroom Displays. Retrieved January 3, 2016, from http://classroomdisplays.org.uk/displays-advice/basics-of-classroom-displays/displaymakerstoolbox/.

6. Sweeney, J. (2010). "3D Bulletin Boards." Clutter-Free Classroom Blog. Retrieved January 3, 2016, from http://littlestlearners.blogspot.com/2010/04/title-featured-friday_30.html.

7. Wikipedia contributors (2005). "Rule of Thirds." Wikipedia, the Free Encyclopedia. Retrieved January 3, 2016, from http://en.wikipedia.org/wiki/Rule_of_thirds.

8. N.A. (2014). Cereal Box Book Report.pdf—Oxford Preparatory Academy. Retrieved September 21, 2014, from https://chino.oxfordchampions.org/media/uploads/redactor/files/5265d633ed1f2Cereal_Box_Book_Report.pdf.

9. Anderson, C. (2014). "Monday Made It: Getting Bulletin Boards Started!" The Teacher Studio. Retrieved September 28, 2014, from http://www.theteacherstudio.com/2014/07/monday-made-it-getting-bulletin-boards.html.

Chapter 4

Student Seating Configurations

School classrooms should have no bad seat.

—Franklin Hill, designer, Disney Celebration School

Guiding Questions

- What seating configuration fits best with your preferred activities? Why?
- What type of activities does the island model support?
- What advantages do tables have over chairs?

DON'T SETTLE FOR JUST ONE SEATING LAYOUT

That three student seating configurations are the most commonly used—the row-and-column model, the island model, and the horseshoe/double horse-shoe model[1]—should not be taken as a sign that there is agreement about which seating arrangements are the best. However, we do believe, as this chapter will illustrate, that students benefit when the seating layout shifts to accommodate the following:

1. The lesson objectives and activities
2. The maturity, energy, and preference of the students
3. Teacher preference
4. Clear sightlines for everyone
5. Design challenges of the room (too small, too narrow, oddly shaped, etc.)
6. Communication between the teacher and students, and among peers

The last consideration, communication, may be the most important in that seating methods either promote or prohibit high to low levels of interaction/ communication. Remember, just because you use one seating layout does not mean you're locked into that particular design. In fact, many instructors use as many as three different setups in a single ninety-minute class.

We should note that most of the research on this subject was conducted in the field of higher education; far fewer studies focused on K-12 classrooms. Such is the case for James McCroskey and Rod McVetta's seminal *Communication Education* article, "Classroom Seating Arrangements: Instructional Communication Theory versus Student Preferences," which reviewed the literature on classroom seating configurations. There is ample evidence to support the following assertions, according to McCroskey and McVetta:

Straight rows

- When struggling students move to the front of straight rows, their academic work improves. However, when strong students move from the front to the back of a room in the same setup, their academic performance does not weaken.
- Students with communication apprehension prefer arrangements that minimize peer-to-peer interaction: straight rows.
- Most interaction between the teacher and students in straight rows occurs in the front and middle section of the seating and diminishes toward the back of the room.

Semicircle formation

- Students sitting directly across from the teacher in a semicircle design experience the most interaction with the instructor.

Island design

- When the island formation is used, students sitting at the head or foot of a table participate in large numbers.

Strange results emerge from the research on classroom seating. The nature of a course whether it is elective or nonelective—determines students' preference for a certain design. Students in elective courses prefer the horseshoe design (see Figure 4.1). When the course is nonelective, they prefer rows.[2] Importantly, we still don't know definitively whether seating creates more or

Figure 4.1 A high school computer class benefits from its large space. Students can switch from collaboration and presentation work in the middle seats (on the left) to individual computer work. *Source*: Jason Korreck.

less participation or if students who choose certain seats naturally participate in large numbers.

One way to take advantage of any seating layout is for the teacher to conscientiously shift her position throughout the class, monitor learners carefully, and call on as many different students as possible. Two apps can help with this:

1. *Teacher's Pick*, an iOS app, gives instructors a novel way to randomly choose students without having to rely on memory. Teacher's Pick keeps track of which students are active, inactive (already chosen), or absent and provides options to pick a student from the active group or pick from the full group (active or inactive). At the end of the day, just click a button and all of the students present are returned to active status (http://appcrawlr. com/ios/teachers-pick).
2. *Stick Pick*, an Android and iOS app, lets you call on a "student at random with just a tap, swipe, or shake" (http://appcrawlr.com/ios/stick pick).

SEATING MODELS

In this section, you'll learn about the strengths and weaknesses of many seating arrangements, from traditional to unorthodox. To enable you to choose the best layout for your classroom, we invite you to consider the following prompts, inspired by W. Michael Kelly's *Rookie Teaching for Dummies*:

- Do you use the projection screen, whiteboard, or chalkboard often? Are there other parts of the room where students need to have clear sightlines?
- Where do you like to plant yourself? At the front of the class? Middle? Will your chosen design afford you enough space?
- How many students have disabilities that require more room, or necessitate their sitting close to you in order to see or hear information?
- Do you interact with students from afar? Or do you like physical proximity to individual students? The latter requires wider aisles.

After setting up your room in the desired configuration, sit down in various seats. Can you get in and out of a student seat without bumping into another chair? Can you move up and down the aisles easily? Can everyone see the board? Then, sit at the instructor's desk. Can you see every seat in the room? If the answer is not yes to all the aforementioned questions, you need to make further adjustments.

Traditional Rows

Military cadets, Broadway fans, movie buffs, and most first to twelfth graders around the world sit in rows (see Figure 4.2). What all these groups and individuals have in common is that the environment expects certain behaviors: for participants to attend to whatever is located at the front of the room, and a good degree of orderliness. Why is straight row arrangement so popular? Maybe because of legacy or perhaps because custodians prefer sweeping between rows. Below are some pros and cons associated with this layout:

Pros

- Traditional rows communicate authority and compliance, which some—but not all—teachers consider a prerequisite to learning.
- Reduces talking, compared the island model where students face each other.
- One of the best models for test taking, because rows thwart cheating more than many other configurations.

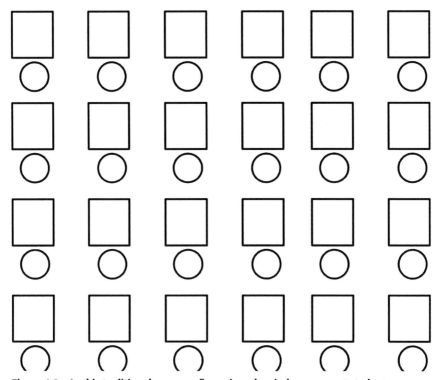

Figure 4.2   In this traditional rows configuration, the circles represent students; squares represent desks. *Source*: Image by Finley & Wiggs.

- Minimizes disruptive student-to-student chatter.
- Supports presentations/lectures because the focus is primarily directed at one speaker.

Cons

- John Dewey, the education philosopher, believed that this layout made student-centered activities difficult to facilitate.
- If there is interaction, the teacher tends to spend more time interacting with the students in the front and middle rows. Not surprisingly, when made to switch their seats to the front of the row, students in the back seat performed better on achievement tests.[3]
- Collaboration is cumbersome.
- Students sitting in the middle and back of a large class are difficult for the instructor to observe.
- Moving between narrow rows is awkward.

Double Columns

A slight twist on the traditional rows is the *double column model,* an arrangement that takes up less space and improves the ability for peers to collaborate with elbow partners. See Figure 4.3.

Island Model

H. Douglas Brown, a researcher at San Francisco State University, advocates for a cooperative learning approach to teaching and learning, a framework that is supported by the student-centered *island* seating model (see Figure 4.4). He writes that cooperative learning classes "encourage students to work together, and to talk to each other in order to achieve specific goals."

Russian psychologist Lev Vygotsky posited that students learn for social reasons. If you agree with that tenet of learning, then this design might be the best for your class. A high school teacher in Baltimore loves the *island* model: "It is so much easier to monitor [student] behavior because you are handling groups of maybe four to five instead of individual students that can sometimes be up to twenty-four."

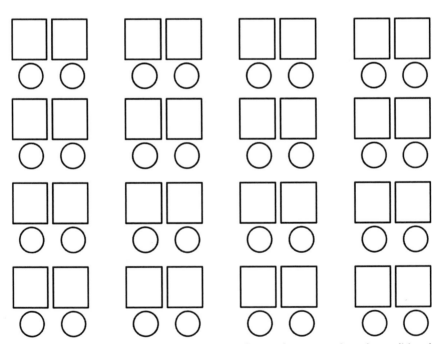

Figure 4.3 The double column arrangement takes up less space than the traditional straight rows model. *Source*: Image by Finley & Wiggs.

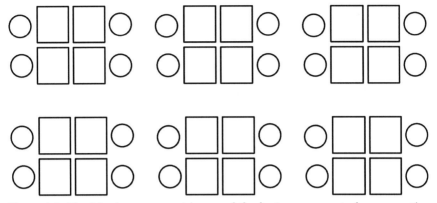

Figure 4.4 The island arrangement is one of the best arrangements for cooperative learning. *Source*: Image by Finley & Wiggs.

Pros

- Increases communication, reflection, and problem solving among the students and allows the teacher to work more closely with individuals and groups. (Savvy instructors carefully choose the groups so that strong students are sitting by weaker ones, and so there are diverse genders and cultures present.)
- Custodians can sweep or mop more quickly when the chairs are stacked on top of the desks.

Cons

- Can increase noise, off-task behavior, and disciplinary referrals, especially among distractible kids.
- Some groups may become too competitive. Warning students that you will frequently change the group members can offset this factor. To randomize group members quickly, use Random Lists (www.Randomlists.com/team-generator).
- Some learners will need to crane their necks to see the teacher.
- Special procedures are required to distribute materials.

Banquet

Similar to the island model, the *banquet* model (see Figure 4.5) employs round tables. Also similar is the *cabaret* arrangement (Figure 4.6), which takes up more room but allows students to face the front of the room.

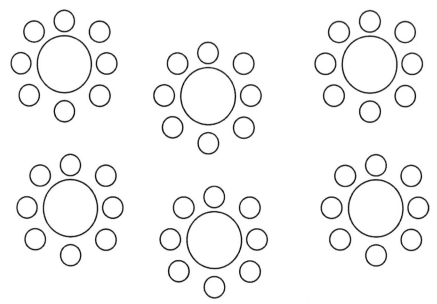

Figure 4.5 The banquet model has many of the advantages and disadvantages of the island arrangement. *Source*: Image by Finley & Wiggs.

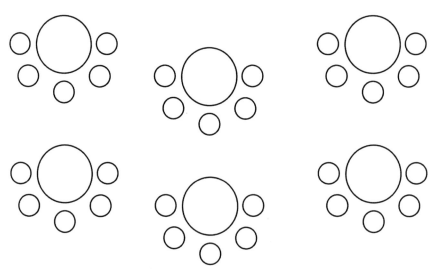

Figure 4.6 The cabaret model is similar to the island model, but students don't have to crane their necks to see the presenter. *Source*: Image by Finley & Wiggs.

Double Horseshoe (or U-Shape)

This semicircle-inspired design (Figure 4.7) works well for teachers who want easy access to individual students or the entire group.

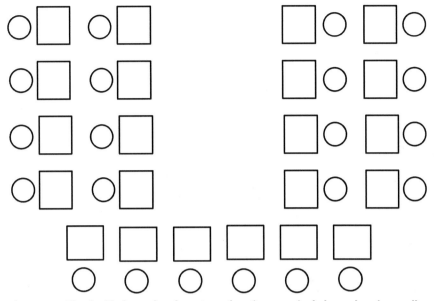

Figure 4.7   The double horseshoe layout can function as a single horseshoe for smaller classes. *Source*: Image by Finley & Wiggs.

Pros

- Works well with small class sizes.[4]
- Like the circle arrangement, it supports activities where students need clear sightlines to one another.
- Partner work is easy to facilitate.
- Some research suggests that this model results in improved student performance and decreased misbehavior.[5]
- Educator Greg Harrison writes enthusiastically about the horseshoe (he calls it the "Upside Down Double U") formation:

  In my mind, this arrangement gives you the best of both worlds; your students will be focused on their work, rather than on each other (the main problem with table groups), and they can easily interact with each other in small groups when they need to [and] your classroom can still feel "open," even with numerous desks.[6]

Cons

- Because there is a large empty space in the middle, some rooms are too small for this model.

- Unruly learners may distract each other, given that there are clear sightlines between a large number of students.
- Small group work is difficult.

Angela Watson, a teacher and blogger, added two islands in the middle of the horseshoe to take advantage of that space. This format, shown below, allows Watson to easily approach any student (see Figure 4.8).

Circle

The circle configuration (Figure 4.9) works for rap sessions, knights in the Arthurian court, and Socratic seminars.

Pros

- Everyone is at the same eye level, even the teacher, which encourages participation.
- All students can easily see each other, an ideal situation for a whole class discussion or any activity where every student is required to speak.

Cons

- Introverted students may feel exposed and vulnerable.

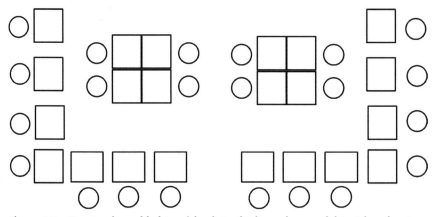

Figure 4.8   One teacher added two islands to the horseshoe model to take advantage of the unused space. *Source*: Image by Finley & Wiggs.

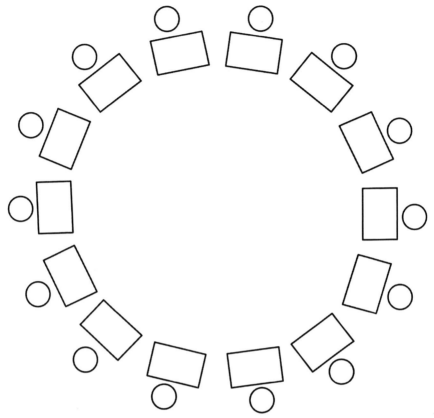

Figure 4.9 Circle seating arrangements support whole class conversations. *Source*: Image by Finley & Wiggs.

Stadium Seating (Angled Rows)

Stadium seating, with angled rows and desks close or touching, keeps students' eyes focused on the front of the class (Figure 4.10).

Pros

- Takes up less floor space than the traditional row model.
- To transition into group activities, learners can simply turn their chairs around to face peers or engage with an elbow partner.
- Easily accommodates an LCD projector and laptop cart.

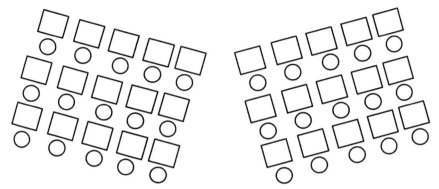

Figure 4.10 Stadium seating saves more space than traditional rows and still keeps students eyes up front. *Source*: Image by Finley & Wiggs.

Cons

- Giving assistance to a learner seated in the middle of the second row is cumbersome.
- Heavily built students may feel crowded unless they are seated at the end of a row.

Unorthodox Models

Do you like to experiment with seating arrangements? If so, the following more unorthodox models might surprise your students when they enter your classroom: *The Double E* (Figure 4.11), *Tables Facing In, Facing Forward* (Figure 4.12), and *Big Center Aisle* (Figure 4.13).

So, which desk arrangements do students prefer? One study suggested that in smaller undergraduate classes, students preferred . . . *wait for it* . . . the horseshoe configuration.[7]

SEATING

Tables or Chairs?

A 2010 study of high school students showed that students preferred tables and chairs to the chair-desk combination; students said that the tables allowed for easier interactions and discussions.[8] Students stated that they did not like how the chair-desks constrained their movements.

When a 2013 study, this time surveying undergraduate students, was commissioned to learn student preference for five seating styles (modern mobile

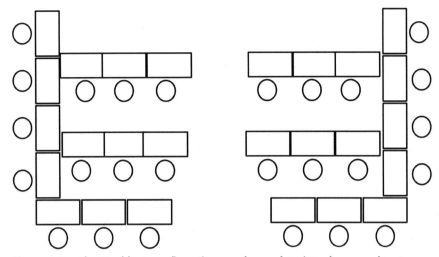

Figure 4.11 The Double E configuration can be used to introduce novelty. *Source*: Image by Finley & Wiggs.

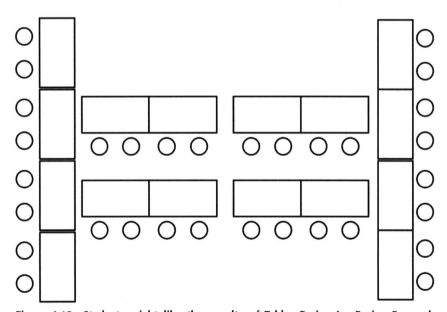

Figure 4.12 Students might like the novelty of Tables Facing In, Facing Forward. *Source*: Image by Finley & Wiggs.

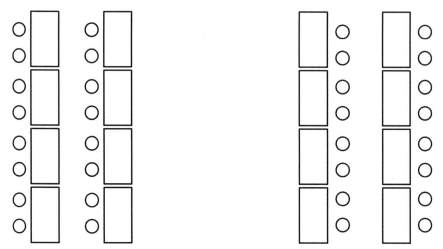

Figure 4.13 The Big Center Aisle layout promotes whole class discussions. *Source*: Image by Finley & Wiggs.

Figure 4.14 A South Central High School teacher finds that the layout pictured accommodates large class sizes. *Source*: Image by Finley & Wiggs.

chairs, tablet arm chairs, fixed tiered seating with tablet arms, rectangle tables with standard chairs, and trapezoid tables with chairs on casters), learners gave *modern mobile chairs* and *trapezoid tables with chairs on casters* high ratings.

One student participant in the study made an enlightening comment: "I have mobility issues and cannot get my scooter into the room. The seats in the classroom made it difficult for me to move around in the classroom."[9]

Seating Configuration Apps

As mentioned in chapter 2, three apps can help you brainstorm some general seating arrangements: *Smart Seat,* by Cornwall, for iOS devices; *Be Seated*, by Jellyfish Pi, for iOS devices; and *Safety Attendance*, by For Safety Solutions, for Android devices. Grid-lined paper and pencil also work well.

Alternatives to Chairs

While alternatives to the typical classroom chair exist, some require that students bring a clipboard with them in order to write on a hard surface.

- *Adirondack Chairs*—Made of wood or plastic, it consists of a fluted back and has wide armrests.
- *Bean Bag Chairs*—A large fabric bag, stuffed with polystyrene beads, that conforms to the user's shape.
- *Couches*
- *Stools*
- *Hokki Stools*—These mushroom-like stools sway from side to side, allowing kids to move while sitting still. They're also stackable, lightweight, and durable.
- *Moon Chairs*—These padded, saucer-shaped chairs are easy to clean.
- *Pillows*
- *Rocking Chairs*
- *Stability Balls*—Made of puncture-resistant elastic and filled with air, they were once thought to engage the abdominal and back muscles, but there are no scientifically verified benefits.
- *Swinging Chair Hammocks*—Made of canvas and held up by rope attached to a wood frame, this chair attaches to the ceiling.

One of our favorite chairs for active learning is designed by IDEO. Under $300, the Steelcase Node School Chair is mobile, swivels, has a storage area underneath the seat for books and bags, contains a small personal surface that swivels with the student and adjusts to different sized bodies, can be used equally well with right- and left-handed students, and is made of flexible plastic that accommodates movement.

SPECIAL CIRCUMSTANCES

Classroom management

If you aren't assigning seats at the beginning of the semester, you're giving up a powerful tool for breaking up potential sources of social resistance to your agenda. Students who are typically off-task often exhibit more academically positive dispositions when they are seated by well-behaved peers or near the instructor.

Getting Students Involved

Since room design is ostensibly for the purpose of supporting youths, shouldn't we ask students to contribute their classroom layout preferences? A New York inclusion teacher, quoted in *Teach-nology*, suggests a method to solicit students' design input:

> Divide the students into four groups and ask each group to come up with a plan that displays an arrangement that everyone in their group is satisfied with. Ask a volunteer from each group to report out to the whole group. Vote on the arrangement that is suited to meet the needs of all.[10]

FAQS ABOUT SEATING

1. *What if students protest their assigned seats?*
   The reptilian brain takes a couple weeks to orient to a new location. Once students establish their territory, their resistance will diminish.
2. *How do you remove relatively new gum from student desks?*
   Put ice cubes in Ziploc bags. Then, let the bag sit on the gum until it becomes brittle and comes off with a knife.
3. *What can be done to reduce the noise of desks scraping across the floor?*
   Nobody wants to listen to thirty-five desks scrape against the linoleum all day. Cut a small hole in the top of a tennis ball and insert the feet of the chairs. Now desks slide silently. Buy cheap off-brand tennis balls or take your family to search the woods next to a tennis court. You'll easily find enough used tennis balls to outfit all the chairs in your classroom.
4. *Should cell phones be allowed on the desk?*

Because smartphones are sophisticated learning tools, they belong on the desk, but they should be set on "airplane mode" and turned upside down until a legitimate academic purpose for them arises.

FINAL THOUGHTS

Although Safa Zerin, in a 2009 study of classroom management and seating configurations, found seating layout to be one of the most important factors in creating a positive learning environment,[11] research on the effect of specific seating layouts on academic performance is still inconclusive.[12] We, therefore, recommend that you experiment with different arrangements and poll your students on their preferences.[13,14]

Find more resources, images, and links related to this chapter at http://www.todd-finley.com/classroom-design-chapt-4-student-seating-configurations/.

NOTES

1. (2011). Assorted Seating Configurations. Retrieved May 23, 2015, from https://www.effectiveteaching.com/product_images/uploaded_images/gobe_120_assorted.pdf.

2. McCroskey J. C., and McVetta, R. (2003). Classroom Seating Arrangements. Retrieved May 23, 2015, from http://www.jamescmccroskey.com/publications/82.htm.

3. J. Daum, as cited by E. Brophy and L. Good, *Teacher-Student Relationships: Causes and Consequences* (New York: Holt, Rinehart, and Winston, 1974), pp. 22–23.

4. Brown, H. D. (2007). *Teaching by Principles: An Interactive Approach to Language Pedagogy* (3rd ed., pp. 40–61).

5. Seating Arrangements for Students—Teach-nology. Retrieved May 29, 2015, from http://www.teach-nology.com/ideas/seating/.

6. McCroskey J. C., and McVetta, R. (2003). Classroom Seating Arrangements. Retrieved May 23, 2015, from http://www.jamescmccroskey.com/publications/82.htm.

7. (2011). Assorted Seating Configurations. Retrieved May 23, 2015, from https://www.effectiveteaching.com/product_images/uploaded_images/gobe_120_assorted.pdf.

8. (2011). Classroom Seating: Which Arrangement Is Best? | Lesson . . . Retrieved June 4, 2015, from http://www.lessonplanet.com/article/education/classroom-seating-which-arrangement-is-best.

9. Heston, J., & Garner, P. "A Study of Personal Spacing and Desk Arrangement in the Learning Environment." Paper presented at the annual convention of the International Communication Association, Atlanta, 1972.

10. Uline, C. L., Wolsey, T. D., Tschannen-Moran, M., & Lin, C. (2010). Improving the Physical and Social Environment of School: A Quest of Equity. *Journal of School Leadership*, 20, 597–632.

11. Harvey, E. J., & Kenyon, M. C. (2013). Classroom Seating Considerations for 21st Century Students and Faculty. *Journal of Learning Spaces*, 2(1). Retrieved from http://libjournal.uncg.edu/jls/article/view/578/454.

12. Seating Arrangements for Students—Teach-nology. Retrieved May 29, 2015, from http://www.teach-nology.com/ideas/seating/.

13. Zerin, S. (2009). *Classroom Management: Seating Arrangements in EFL Classrooms*. Dhaka: Brac University.

14. Meeks, M. D., Knotts, T. L., James, K. D., Williams, F., Vassar, J. A., & Wren, A. O. (2013). The Impact of Seating Location and Seating Type on Student Performance. *Education Sciences*, 3(4), 375–386.

Chapter 5

Extending the Classroom
Blended Learning

Digital learning means not being confined to brick and mortar classrooms.

—Mark Quinn

Guiding Questions

- What model of blended learning would work best for my classroom?
- How do I design an effective online learning space?
- What do I need to remember when designing modules?
- How do I transition students from online to face-to-face learning environments?

HOW DO YOU CHOOSE WHICH ONLINE TOOL IS THE BEST?

Make no mistake, education technology dramatically disrupts traditional institutions, roles, and the limitations of the four-walled physical classroom. Furthermore, the merger of online space and face-to-face (FTF) instruction has created educational tools that are unique to the twenty-first century—tools that can solve multiple challenges facing students—by making highly qualified teachers more available, increasing access to courses not offered by a school, and enhancing personalized learning opportunities.

With so many tech tools and hybrid platforms to choose from, answering the following questions might help you make a decision about which ones will work best for you:

- What are your needs and technology competencies?
- What is your budget for tech?
- What technologies are already available to your classroom?
- What are your students' learning needs?
- What tech is commonly associated with your discipline?
- What tech support is available?

Regardless of your level of adventurousness, you'll have to keep learning about technology because it's always changing. Vicki Davis, a Georgia teacher, plays with a new technology every day for thirty minutes during lunch. She realizes that education technology is here to stay and has therefore adopted the daily exploration habit.

DESIGNING YOUR BLENDED LEARNING SPACE

Choosing a Learning Management System (LMS)

We interviewed Mark Samberg, the technological innovations project manager at the William and Ida Friday Institute, which employs cutting-edge research and cross-sector collaboration between education, government, and private industries to help schools become future-oriented organizations. Mark advises teachers to pick an LMS that works across all your devices, is simple to use, and fits your instructional model. He also recommends picking one that makes it easy to import and export data so that the content is reusable and that allows teachers to exchange learning objects as they collaboratively plan. Finally, he advises picking one that provides extensive cloud storage.

Although not comprehensive, the following is a list of noteworthy LMSs:

1. *Canvas*—A user-friendly and feature-rich LMS, this platform is a current darling of many reviewers, in part, because it works well with other devices and programs.
2. *Google Classroom*—This LMS is available to anyone with Google Apps for Education and helps teachers create and manage student assignments.
3. *Moodle*—Setup of this open source platform is simple and the interface is easy to manage. Options for customization are more limited than other LMSs.
4. *Blackboard*—With extensive options, Blackboard is the default LMS for many universities.

5. *Schoology*—Possessing an interface similar to Facebook, this platform works well on different screens: smartphones, tablets, notebook computers, and desktops.
6. *Haiku Learning*—This LMS has a highly customizable newspaper-like interface. Teachers report that grading assignments within the tool is a snap.
7. *Sakai*—Created by educators for educators, this tool is a fully open source and a popular choice for university professors.

Regardless of which LMS you choose, build in time to experiment and improve the student experience. Megan List, who taught social studies in a 1:1 technology initiative, shared her experiences with us:

> I set up Moodle on my computer and had the students accessing their assignments digitally. To expand that, we used Ning (a group-based social networking platform) and Twitter. I was really just feeling my way through and making stuff up.

Developing online learning spaces was and still is pioneer work. Fortunately, the knowledge base has expanded. Below, we summarize Woolley-Wilson, Hudson, Green, & Kerns's "6 Models of Blended Learning"[1]:

- *Face-to-Face Driver Model:* This approach to blended learning is used when instruction is mostly delivered in a traditional format, but online learning is used for remediation and/or supplemental resources to better individualize instruction for students. This model is often seen in heterogeneous classrooms where online instruction is used for remediation, intervention, or enrichment. To summarize the Face-to-Face Driver Model: *Traditional Instruction + Online Remediation and Supplemental Resources.*
- *Rotation Model:* Similar to the Face-to-Face Driver Model, this approach (frequently used in elementary school settings) requires students to be located in the same building as their teachers throughout the day. Learners move through variations of teacher-led instruction, online instruction, and collaborative group-work. To summarize: *Rotation Model = Tech "Stations" Approach.*
- *Flex Model:* In this model, instruction occurs primarily online; personalized learning allows students to move into areas of interest and need. The approach is popular with at-risk students who have difficulty in traditional learning contexts. Although instruction is primarily delivered online, the teacher of record provides individual support and facilitates group projects and assignments. To summarize this approach: *Mostly Online Learning + Minimal FTF Instructor Support.*

- *Online Lab Model:* In this model, the entire course is delivered online, but students are located in a classroom on campus. To summarize: *Online Lab = 100% Online Learning.*
- *Self-Blend Model:* In order to have access to classes not offered in traditional high schools, students enroll in remote online courses. To summarize: *Traditional FTF Learning + Extra Online Learning.*
- *Online Driver Model:* Information is primarily delivered online and students can check in with the teacher if needed. To summarize: *Online Learning + Online Instructor.*

Many teachers supplement their LMS choices with free online tools that improve *communication, community, and collaboration.*

- *TodaysMeet*—A technology used as a backchannel (a secondary conversation that occurs at the same time as a lecture or activity), TodaysMeet is a disposable and private chat space for students to ask questions, provide resources, and express their thoughts without disrupting the classroom flow.
- *Mentimeter*—Gathers data from your students in real time and displays the data as visual information.
- *Twitter*—A microblog platform that limits posts to 140 characters, Twitter allows students to use (#) hashtags to represent various classes, concepts, projects, and assignments.
- *Padlet*—A free virtual corkboard, Padlet allow multiple users to post multimedia notes simultaneously.
- *Blogs*—A weblog that consists of posts appearing in reverse chronological order, a blog is a popular platform for millions of writers. Our favorites are Wordpress, Medium, and Blogger.
- *Google Docs*—Fifty students at one time can collaboratively edit a web-based document.
- *Collaborize Classroom*—A free site, Collaborize is password-protected and has built-in assessment modules.

Choosing the best free communication, community, and collaboration tool is often a matter of trial and error, as coauthor Blake and his colleague John Suralik discovered when they were charged with conjoining their two classrooms, twenty-three miles apart. Their resources included two web cameras, two microphones, and a Skype account—later upgraded to a Polycom system.

To make technology decisions, John and Blake talked through these critical questions:

- How can we use free, available technologies to maximize the effects of synchronous instruction?

- How do we enhance FTF instruction and make both classrooms feel like one environment?
- What learning experiences do we want our students to have?

Both instructors liked the Socratic seminar model. But they also wanted to increase student engagement by creating a Fishbowl (double circle) dialogue between both classrooms. So, they decided that the inside discussion circle would consist of four students from each class, chatting orally with microphones and video; the remaining students (twenty-one in each class) would use a backchannel to annotate the discussion (see Figure 5.1).

Through experimentation with Wikispaces, then TodaysMeet, they finally settled on Collaborize Classroom to support online "discussion," a tool that could report on the # of student posts and replies, so that the instructors didn't have to count them by hand. Former student Abigail Snooks said that debates were more honest "because we didn't have to see the other students every day. We were more honest when debating controversial topics."

Blake and John leveraged backchannel communication tools in order to create pathways between the digital and physical space so that the two environments complemented each other like two functional and organized rooms in the same well-designed house.

Similarly, experimentation and invention can occur when trying to make the online and physical learning spaces complementary. Twenty-first-century collaboration in both spaces was important to William Burgess, an Earth Science teacher at Wake STEM Early College High School. So, he attached a

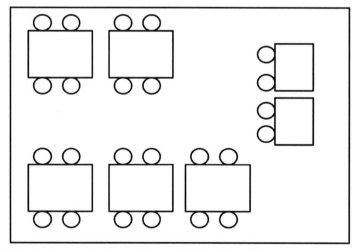

Figure 5.1 A diagram depicting John and Blake's hybrid Socratic seminar. *Source:* Image by Finley & Wiggs.

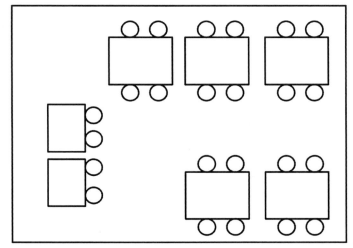

Figure 5.2 A Wake STEM Early College High School teacher attached Televisions to Steelcase tables to maximize student-to-student collaboration in the physical and digital spaces. *Source:* William Burgess.

46" TV to Steelcase tables to maximize student-to-student collaboration (see Figure 5.2).

MODULE DESIGN

An online module organizes a semester of classes into a week of time— though some modules span greater time periods. Generally, modules include reading assignments, online discussion forum prompts, tasks to complete, projects, e-papers, and quizzes. Although there is no best option, learning modules often share many of the characteristics outlined below:

1. Title of the module
2. Dates when the module is active (dates are typically one week at a time)
3. Overview
   a. Introduction and context (conveyed through friendly, but specific language)
      i. A video or audio recording of the instructor's voice
      ii. A couple of written paragraphs describing the module
   b. Objectives
      i.   Objectives are specific and actionable
      ii. Objectives should align with the formative and summative assessments
      iii. Tie each objective to specific assignments and assessments

    c. List of assignments the student will need to complete
       i. Provide a clearly understood title for each assignment
      ii. Associate a specific date and time that each assignment is due, and how it should be submitted
     iii. Assign numeric values (a specific number of points or a specific percentage of the course grade) to each assignment
     iv. Include scoring rubrics that will be used to grade the assignments
    d. Identification of technology the student will be using in the module
       i. Software (e.g., Microsoft Word, PowerPoint, etc.)
      ii. Online tools (e.g., Voicethread, Google Drive, TodaysMeet, etc.)
    e. Estimated time required for students to complete the module
    f. Notification of the instructor's availability to offer assistance via phone, email, discussion board, Skype, or Google Hangouts
4. Content and formative assessment (instructor-recorded videos, readings, audio recordings, YouTube, Jing walk-throughs of content, uploaded PowerPoint, online readings, chapters needing to be read in a purchased e-book or textbook, etc.)
5. Summarization
6. Summative Assessment
    a. Quizzes (with point values identified)
    b. Essays (with scoring rubrics and point values identified)
    c. Performance tasks (with scoring rubrics and point values identified)
7. Date/Time when the next module opens
    a. Include the title of the next module in the context of the entire course outline
    b. Provide links to the course syllabus, the online gradebook, and to the next module in the sequence

Modules offer multiple parallels to the FTF world, such as presentation tools and synchronous communication via Google Docs, Mural.ly, Padlet, Stixy, TodaysMeet, GroupZap, MindMeister, and Wikis.

Reducing Cognitive Load

Learners will want to process through your module as quickly as possible, but slow enough to comprehend the content, instructions, and assessments. If directions are confusing, assignments don't make sense. If learners are not sure where to click, frustration kicks in and adds to *cognitive load*—the mental effort that taxes working memory. More load, less learning.

    In the same way that textbook authors include chapter overviews, graphic organizers, headings and subheadings, fonts of key terms in bold and cursive, images, reflection questions, pull quotes, reviews, and chapter summaries, designers of online learning spaces also need to signal to the learner which concepts, definitions, instructions, and readings are more important than others.

You might think all of your content is important. However, if not given a sense of which content the instructor values more than others, the online student is likely to read every word in your module yet remain somewhat confused about the key takeaways. Content that is (a) simplified, (b) requires students to reflect, or (c) has learners apply the content to solve a problem has a greater chance of being remembered.

So, when creating the module, add features that signal to the reader when they should make a metacognitive shift:

1. When does the module suggest that skimming or reading fast might be appropriate?
2. Will the learner understand the general outline of a module—benefited by summaries, graphic organizers, headings and subheadings?
3. Does the user have a place to go when he or she is confused, such as a discussion forum, glossary, or index?
4. Can a learner scan a module and get the gist of the critical concepts and ideas?
5. Are the images mere decorations, or do they help the student understand a concept?

Finally, every online learner should have a sense of what the significant takeaways are—the answer to *so what?* This can be communicated graphically or through narrative. This last point will be expanded upon in the following section.

Visual Cues

Good graphic design has the effect of decreasing an individual's cognitive load. Whether you are organizing a classroom blog, website, or LMS, it is important to adhere to the principles of graphic design to ensure users are engaging with the content rather than overtaxing their brains trying to decipher the design of the module.

Consider the following visual cue principles that Garr Reynolds describes in *Presentation Zen Design: Simple Design Principles and Techniques to Enhance Your Presentations*:

Rule No. 1: Contrast—Take into consideration how size, color, location, spacing, and shape reinforce and distract from the big content takeaways.

Studies suggest that the following design choices significantly impact learning and knowledge retention—again, by decreasing cognitive load:

- Contrasting the text and background colors
- Using a legible font (particularly fonts designed for on-screen reading)
- Avoiding "busy" visuals
- Using white space liberally (and intentionally to guide the reader)
- Providing visual cues with images, graphics, and animations.

Content should be easy to read, and significant content needs to stand out to the learner in a way that is not distracting.

Rule No. 2: Repetition—When creating multiple module pages or slides, be consistent. For example, use the same background, color, font, and font size from one slide to the next. Providing a consistent framework with repeated visual and text cues puts the learner at ease.

Rule No. 3: Alignment—We need order in our lives. When an online learning space is organized logically, it gives the student confidence that the module design is purposeful and can be successfully completed. There are two types of alignment to consider: (a) alignment of margins, text, and images and (b) objectives, assessments, and instructional strategies. Ask yourself these key questions to ensure you are following the principles of alignment:

- *Objectives*—What do learners need to know, understand, and do? How are these objectives aligned to Bloom's Taxonomy or to other learning frameworks?
- *Assessments*—Are your assessments aligned with the goals, objectives, and content? Can the goals and objectives be assessed through a multiple-choice test, or is it more appropriate to create a performance-based assessment?
- *Instructional Approach*—How will you deliver instruction in a way that maintains pedagogical fidelity from one module to the next?

Rule No. 4: Proximity—It is useful to consider how you have sequenced content. Students intuitively assume that when content is in visual proximity to other content, those ideas are more closely related—even when that is not the designer's intention.[2]

The key point to remember about Garr Reynolds's design rules is this: think deliberately about where module components should go and how they should look to help students have an intuitive and pleasant user experience.

FINAL THOUGHTS

As long as your decisions about online spaces, tools, and design keep students' needs at the forefront, you can't go wrong. We agree with Secretary of Education Arne Duncan, when he discussed the "new normal" of using technology to do more with less in public education:

> Better use of online learning, virtual schools, and other smart uses of technology is not so much about replacing educational roles as it is about giving each person the tools they need to be more successful—reducing wasted time, energy, and money.[3]

Find more resources, images, and links related to this chapter at http://www. todd-finley.com/design-book-chapt-5-extending-the-classroom-blended-learning/.

NOTES

1. Woolley-Wilson, J., Hudson, T., Green, N., & Kerns, D. (2013, October 23). 6 Models of Blended Learning—DreamBox Learning. Retrieved June 26, 2015.

2. Reynolds, G. (2010). *Presentation Zen Design: Simple Design Principles and Techniques to Enhance Your Presentations.* Berkeley, CA: New Riders.

3. Duncan, A. (2010, November 17). The New Normal: Doing More with Less—Secretary Arne Duncan's Remarks at the American Enterprise Institute. Retrieved June 26, 2015.

Chapter 6

Classroom Design with Classroom Management in Mind

The greatest sign of success for a teacher is to be able to say,
"the children are now working as if I did not exist."

—Maria Montessori

Guiding Questions

- What is the connection between physical and cognitive space?
- How can classroom organization minimize classroom management issues?
- How do you set up stations in a small classroom?

DESIGN THINKING, ENVIRONMENT, AND CLASSROOM MANAGEMENT

Taking a design thinking approach to addressing issues related to classroom management, the physical space, and student behavior is a natural part of being a reflective practitioner and a disposition that is correlated strongly with success. Design thinking, as discussed in chapter 1, involves

1. Identifying and understanding a problem
2. Looking at the issue from different perspectives
3. Brainstorming solutions
4. Implementing the solutions

These steps are internalized in the thinking routines of instructors who deal effectively with behavior problems. Some teachers think this way with *automaticity*—at the unconscious level—while others need to write out their reflections.

Start with Observing

One of the things that coauthor Blake finds most difficult about moving into a new home is organizing the kitchen in a way that maximizes its functionality for all the members of his household. Just like a classroom, Blake's kitchen is a profoundly collaborative space. It isn't until two or more people begin cooking for the first time that they begin to recognize the inefficiencies involved in where the utensils, pots, knives, plates, Cuisinart, and other items are placed.

Before preparing the first meal, it's hard to predict how idiosyncratic each individual's cooking style is. But the problems become obvious as soon as stakeholders unnecessarily cross paths, or bump shoulders when reaching for seemingly unrelated items. When this happens, people need to rethink how things are organized and revisit procedures for how and when to work together.

The same principles hold true for the classroom. The day before students arrive you might think that your classroom is organized efficiently, and that you've thought through how placement of objects might create bottlenecks or management issues. However, the way kids function in the classroom is difficult to predict with precision.

In other words, it is likely that the physical space that you have organized in a specific way will need to be adjusted based on your observations of how students use the space. In fact, you may need to make adjustments in the space within the first few minutes of class if you see some aspect of the classroom design creating a classroom management issue.

Stronge, Tucker, and Hindman's *Handbook for Qualities of Effective Teachers* describes how little details can trip students up as much as big issues:

> Placing materials near the pencil sharpener may seem like a good idea, until one considers that at the start of a lesson this area may become congested with some students retrieving materials for their group and others waiting to use the pencil sharpener. However, the pencil sharpener and the trashcan may be a good pairing if the pencil sharpener tends to break regularly, spilling its contents on the floor; this way shavings fall into the trash instead. Effective teachers think about the little details that enhance the use of available space in the classroom as well as the big issues.[1]

It might be unclear how putting a trashcan underneath a pencil sharpener enhances classroom management. The point is, the entire classroom space is a system, and making that system frictionless minimizes problems and enhances proacademic behaviors. Being cognizant about how the environment encourages or subverts successful teaching and learning is the first step of the design cycle. So, when students enter the class,

1. *Observe*—Identify and understand situations that hinder successful management of the class.
2. *Get multiple perspectives*—Solicit student feedback. "Is there enough room in that aisle?"
3. *Brainstorm solutions*—"What would help this situation?"
4. *Implement the solution and reassess*—"Let's try Brandi's solution for a couple of days and reassess if we want to keeping using it on Wednesday."

If you make students stakeholders in improving classroom conditions, they will be less likely to view your rules as something to resist.

THINKING THROUGH CLASSROOM ORGANIZATION AND CLASSROOM MANAGEMENT

In the 1970s, airport security checkpoints often had packs of frustrated passengers waiting and jockeying for position. Today, most of the major airport checkpoints have stanchions and retractable belts set up to guide passengers without anyone telling them where to go. Similarly, not having to repeat directions or corrections allows instructors to spend more time teaching content and skills.

> Classroom management and organization are intertwined. While rules and routines influence student behavior, classroom organization affects the physical elements of the classroom, making it a more productive environment for its users. How the classroom environment is organized influences the behavior in it.[2]

Good classroom organization is intuitive, so explanations are only minimally needed. When the physical space is well organized, there are fewer classroom management problems, allowing the teacher to attend to the important stuff: helping students learn content.

KEY DEFINITIONS

The following paragraphs define some of the terms that will help instructors thoughtfully consider the relationship between classroom management and the classroom environment.

Classroom Organization

Classroom organization considers the physical nature of the room. Effective teachers think through and design an environment that supports safety and optimizes learners' performance. They also "strategically place furniture, learning centers, and materials in order to optimize student learning and reduce distractions."[3]

Classroom Management

Classroom management is related to all the choices teachers make—decisions about the physical environment, about activities, and about expectations that create a space where students' academic and emotional well-being is supported. Posted rules and routines support those goals.

> Effective teachers also use rules, procedures, and routines to ensure that students are actively involved in learning (Marzano, Marzano, & Pickering, 2003). In essence, they use management not to control student behavior, but to influence and direct it in a constructive manner to set the stage for instruction (McLeod, Fisher, & Hoover, 2003).[4]

When behaviors that support learning are supported, the classroom climate feels more positive and agentive to learners.

Classroom Routines

Before students enter your classroom, visualize expectations for specific routines, particularly ones that have created classroom management problems in the past. Then, plan out how you will teach the routine to avoid problems. "A classroom routine is simply a well-rehearsed response to a teacher's directive."[5] Routines rely on well-thought-out *procedures*, or "outline specific behaviors during a particular type of activity."[6] The time you take to teach the steps of a procedure saves hassles later.

K. J. Wagner outlines a list of common classroom routines. As you consider each item, put a checkmark by all those that require you to create a poster describing each step and put two checks by those that you'll need to have students rehearse.

- Entering the classroom
- Beginning work
- Roll call/lunch count
- Announcements

- Tardies
- Teacher's attention signal (bell, chime)
- Getting out of your seat
- Getting supplies
- Sharpening pencils
- Procedures for handling equipment
- Getting into/working in groups
- Independent work
- Working at a center
- Lining up to leave the room
- Getting a drink from the water fountain
- Going to the restroom
- Going to the clinic, office, media center, or elsewhere
- Passing in homework or papers
- What to do if you finish work early
- Responding to fire drills, lock downs, tornado alerts, etc.[7]

Classroom Rules

Rules are general expectations of conduct that support teaching and learning. They should "apply to student behavior in all classroom situations, regardless of the activity. In that way, rules are distinct from procedures, which outline specific behaviors during a particular type of activity."[8] When posting rules, avoid the temptation to be general (e.g., *try your best*) and don't list everything you can think of. The ideal amount is four to eight rules, and can include things like:

1. Don't interrupt other students' learning.
2. Come prepared every day with extra pencils, paper, the assigned book.
3. Arrive on time and ready to learn with smartphones put away until the instructor indicates that it is time for them to be used.
4. Use polite language with fellow students and the teacher.

Make sure you have a conversation with students about the rules on the first day of class and tell students that, if necessary, you may add more rules to the list later. Display the rules prominently.

Protocol

Protocols are sequential guidelines that "structure professional conversations or learning experiences to ensure that meeting, planning, or group-collaboration time is used efficiently, purposefully, and productively. The National

School Reform Faculty and the School Reform Initiative are the two primary sources of protocols in the United States, and hundreds of protocols can be downloaded from their websites."[9] Like rules, we recommend that you post protocols in the classroom, give students a hard copy, and send an electronic copy to parents.

Ritual

Across cultures, people in general and students specifically need *rituals*—actions that occur in a prescribed order, that cue thinking and feeling in a way that is conducive to the effective practices of an environment. One example is the Pledge of Allegiance—a routine that is concretized into the physical space by the prominent display of the American Flag. Another example is singing "Happy Birthday" that is baked into the environment with decorated cake or cupcakes.

> In most religious services, the ritual is also highlighted by music, and in some cases, incense. This is, essentially, a multi-sensory approach to helping people learn and feel comfortable with the routine. . . . People's need for this safe, comfortable routine can be seen in the discomfort with changes in those routines, such as the disruption caused by Superstorm Sandy! Classroom rituals and routines can provide children with the same benefits.[10]

Classroom routines should help the community bond and prepare students for learning. For example, coauthor Todd's favorite routine occurs at the beginning of class. He always starts by asking his pupils for good news. This gives learners a chance to share and create a positive association with the class community. He reinforces this activity by always listing "Good News" on the board after "Today's Objectives" in the agenda section of the whiteboard.

Finally, because routines, procedures, and rules help organize behaviors, feelings, and thinking, we recommend being conscious of how the physical and cognitive space complement each other.[11]

CONFUSION CAUSES CLASSROOM MANAGEMENT PROBLEMS

Confusion leads to problems. If the work is too hard, kids resist. If it's too easy, they become lethargic and crabby. When they don't know what to do or where to go, student behavior grows increasingly unpredictable.

Transitions

As we have discussed, problems are most likely to arise during transitions—times when students are between tasks. Two big transitions occur when students enter and leave the classroom.

You can help diffuse problems in the first seconds of your first class—according to Harry Wong, the author of *The First Days of School*—by distributing to each student a ticket at the door that tells them what their seating section color is and seat number.[12] So, instead of anxiously looking all over the room for their seats and nametags, students spot how five desk groupings each have different colored name tags; they can walk directly to their assigned color and sit down. This shortens transition time and empowers students.

Fortunately, making adjustments in the physical space can facilitate movement from one activity to the next. Here are two tips for expediting common transitions:

- *Magnetized attendance*—One homeroom teacher we know keeps a magnetized board near the class entrance, above the space where students turn in papers. When students arrive each day, they move a magnet with their name to one of two columns labeled with a preference: *dogs or cats, grilled cheese or ham sandwich, Diet Coke or real Coke, Paris or Rome, cake or pie, etc.* Students enjoy voting and seeing if their preferences align with peers. After all the kids have voted, the magnetized names left on the bottom of the board are marked as absent.
- *Lining up indicators*—Place subtle marks on the floor where students are to stand when lining up. This reduces the chance of bumps leading to fisticuffs.
- *Cooperative group transitions*—If students are transitioning from independent work to group work, knowing where and how to move, and what to do once they get there, is extremely important. Teach these movements like you're part traffic cop, part ballet instructor. Students should know which direction they should move, how fast, whether they are trading seats or moving their own chair, and how far apart the desks should be. Too many cooperative groups have one or more students sitting far enough out of the team circle that not everyone can hear and fully participate in the work.

When teaching transitions, explain the reason why the transition needs a procedure, walk through the do's and don'ts of the procedure, model the procedure while being super explicit and animated so that students remember the instructions. Finally, only teach procedures when you think there might be problems that would occur otherwise.

The biggest—and often overlooked—transition occurs when the teacher is absent. All teachers should have substitute materials located in a tub or packet, filled with the following: the bell schedule, office passes, classroom management protocols and behavior referrals, the "designated student substitute assistant," and a big bottle of aspirin (as a joke). We also recommend providing a photo of each class with names written under the faces, so that the substitute knows where students should be sitting and what their names are.

ORGANIZE MATERIALS TO REDUCE CONFUSION

When students know where to find materials and how to interact with them, they're more likely to engage in proacademic behaviors. Confusion eats away at instructional time. We, therefore, recommend the following material management practices:

- Have materials for groups placed in labeled ("Group 1 Materials") tubs or trays before class starts.
- Keep clearly labeled student supplies at a conveniently located station, so that they aren't asking you for tape, scissors, rulers, erasers, the stapler, etc.
- Work out a lost or broken pencil policy. Some teachers keep a can of golf pencils near the pencil sharpener. If a pencil breaks while being sharpened, there is no fuss in finding a replacement.
- Keep a stack of recycled paper at the student supply station.

By organizing and making supplies available, instructors reduce potential conflicts that can arise over stolen pens or students interrupting class to beg peers for paper.

REDUCE ANXIETY WITH CLASSROOM SIGNS

As teachers, our job is to predict and help students effectively navigate academics. Here's how to use the classroom walls to do just that:

- *Post daily objectives*—Use conversational language, if possible, so students understand *what* they're learning.
- *Post essential questions*—These are inquiries related to an important concept covered within a discipline. Answers to these questions help students understand *why* they're learning the day's material.
- *Post agenda items*—This will save you having to tell ten kids what they will be doing in class when they ask.

- *Assignments due dates*—This helps students stay organized.
- *Post rules*—You can't follow the rules unless you know them.
- *Post what students should do when they finish early*—This keeps students focused on academics.
- *Post emergency procedures*—Kids need to know what to do in the event of a tornado, fire, or lockdown warning. Also, clearly mark where the nearest first aid and fire extinguisher is located. Science labs should indicate where the eyewash station and emergency shut-off valves are.
- *Post a dismissal policy*—Do students leave when the bell rings? Line up? Put their chairs up at the end of the day? Clear the floor of scraps of paper before they go?

If each sign features a memorable image, there is a better chance that students will independently notice the sign.

FAQS ABOUT CENTERS

1. *Where should you locate centers in the room?*
   Centers can get loud. Therefore, position centers that have the potential to be the loudest (games, group problem solving) at opposite ends of the room.
2. *Don't problems erupt in centers when kids find the work too hard or easy? Will they goof off?*
   Make sure you have *assignment cards* and materials at each center that are differentiated by ability or multiple intelligences. Also, ensure all students have sheets that they turn in for a grade at the end of the class to make them accountable for visiting all the centers and completing their work. The sheet should ask students to reflect on what they learned at each center.
3. *What if my room is too small for stations?*
   Angela Watson, a former teacher and now a consultant in Brooklyn, pushes students' desks to the middle of the room and positions her stations around the walls.[13]

FINAL THOUGHTS

In the late 1700s, English philosopher and theorist Jeremy Bentham designed a type of prison or insane asylum that allowed a single watchman at the center of the circular interior of a building clear sightlines to every inmate, without those institutionalized being able to tell when they were being observed.

Of course, the official on watch couldn't observe everyone every second of the day, but the threat of being seen effectively gave inmates the sense that they were being watched—they therefore behaved as though they were monitored every moment. In the case of classrooms, we don't want to create an authoritarian Panopticon that kids feel compelled to resist.

We do, however, need to convey that we notice, care about, and want to reward behaviors that are sensitive and generous to the needs of others, and that promote independence. "At the beginning of the year, teachers must set expectations and create a motivational climate for learning and combine this with orchestrating the physical space in order to both create and implement a successful classroom management system."[14]

Find more resources, images, and links related to this chapter at http://www. todd-finley.com/design-book-chapt-6-classroom-management-in-mind/.

NOTES

1. Stronge, J., Tucker, P., & Hindman, J. (2004). Chapter 3. Classroom Management and Organization. In *Handbook for Qualities of Effective Teachers*. Alexandria, VA: Association for Supervision and Curriculum Development.

2. Stronge, J., Tucker, P., & Hindman, J. (2004). Chapter 3. Classroom Management and Organization. In *Handbook for Qualities of Effective Teachers*. Alexandria, VA: Association for Supervision and Curriculum Development.

3. Stronge, J., Tucker, P., & Hindman, J. (2004). Chapter 3. Classroom Management and Organization. In *Handbook for Qualities of Effective Teachers*. Alexandria, VA: Association for Supervision and Curriculum Development.

4. Stronge, J., Tucker, P., & Hindman, J. (2004). Chapter 3. Classroom Management and Organization. In *Handbook for Qualities of Effective Teachers*. Alexandria, VA: Association for Supervision and Curriculum Development.

5. Dr. Fred Jones' Tools for Teaching. (2004). Retrieved June 17, 2015, from http://www.educationworld.com/a_curr/columnists/jones/jones002.shtml.

6. Classroom Management & Culture. (2010). Teach For America. Retrieved June 17, 2015, from http://www.teachingasleadership.org/sites/default/files/Related-Readings/CMC_2011.pdf.

7. Wagner, K. J. (2005). Routines and Procedures for Managing Your Classroom. Retrieved June 17, 2015.

8. Classroom Management & Culture. (2010). Teach For America. Retrieved June 17, 2015, from http://www.teachingasleadership.org/sites/default/files/Related-Readings/CMC_2011.pdf.

9. Protocol Definition. (2013, May 15). Retrieved June 17, 2015, from edglossary.org.

10. Are You Harnessing the Power of Rituals in Your Classroom. (2014). Retrieved June 17, 2015.

11. Classroom Management—Creating a Learning Environment, Setting Expectations, Motivational Climate, Maintaining a Learning Environment, When Problems Occur. (n.d.). Retrieved June 29, 2015, from http://education.stateuniversity.com/pages/1834/Classroom-Management.html.

12. Wong, H. K. (2011). The First Days of School. Retrieved June 17, 2015, from https://www.effectiveteaching.com/products.php?product=The-First-Days-of-School.

13. Watson, A. (2010). Setting Up Centers/Stations. Retrieved June 17, 2015.

14. Classroom Management—Cre.ating a Learning Environment, Setting Expectations, Motivations Climate, Maintaining a Learning Environment, When Problems Occur. (2007). Retrieved June 17, 2015.

Chapter 7

The Teacher's Desk
Conquering Clutter

Simplicity boils down to two steps: Identify the essential. Eliminate the rest.

—Leo Babauta

Guiding Questions

- Why should you have two sets of the same supplies?
- Why do some instructors forgo the teacher's desk?
- What kind of impression do you want your desk to make?

CLASSROOM HEADQUARTERS

The instructor's desk functions as a conference space, first-aid location, grading and planning zone, and area to organize often used materials (glue stick, highlighter, Post-it® & Stickies™ Notes, Scotch® Tape, masking tape, pens, binder clips, rubber bands, room deodorizers, scissors, etc.) so they can be quickly retrieved. It's your home base, so make it reflect aesthetics that invite productivity and showcase what it means to be a content expert.

START FRESH

Before creating the ideal instructor's area, clean out and wash whatever desk you've inherited. Make a pile of all the desk's artifacts and get ready to make decisions. Next, sort each object into four piles:

1. Things used often at your desk.
2. Things you rarely use at your desk.
3. Duplicates (pens, scissors, etc.).
4. Decorations that take up too much of a desk footprint.

Only keep items that fall into category #1. You don't need anything from lines #2–4, so *get rid them*. Recycle old papers, throw away trash, and put everything away in its proper place. If you only need one or two pens for everyday use, donate the rest to your office supply room or to a coworker.

After you clean out the desk, answering these questions will help you make decisions about where to put things:

- What are the materials that you will need to access the most? (Those should be the closest and most accessible.)
- Is the desk for materials that only the teacher will use?
- Will the students interact with your teacher station by
  ○ submitting papers to you at your desk?
  ○ retrieving items like the stapler? bathroom pass? Kleenex? files?
- Do you like having a large number of resources handy or prefer a minimalist sanctuary?
- Will you grade and plan at your desk?
- Will you hold conferences with individuals or small groups of students at your desk?
- Will you use your computer at your desk? (If so, you'll need to make room for a monitor and printer.)
- Are there expensive or sensitive items that need to be locked away, such as a purse, gradebook, or cell phone?

Two zones are common for most professional desktops, according to Martha Stewart: *to do* and *in progress*. But instructors might need more zones than other professionals, such as *grade, return, copy,* and *file*. Each zone should be labeled and defined with a letter tray or file box.

Once your desk is clean and set up, remember these four rules:

1. *Every Object Should Have a Specific Home.* Artifacts should remain there, unless it's in use.
2. *Schedule Regular Cleaning Time*—This will take only a few moments if done every day.
3. *Never Put Trash Down*—Whether it is a piece of paper or a food wrapper, get in the habit of holding it in your hand until you can throw it in the trash.

4. *Take a Picture*—Do you have items on your desk that are simply for reference? Instead of leaving these items on your desk, take pictures with your smartphone. Do you need a hard copy of the school lunch schedule or bus schedule? Not if you take a picture of it with your smartphone camera and send that photo to your Evernote account, a searchable cloud-based storage solution.

The teacher's workspace includes everything that is within reach when you are behind the desk (see Figure 7.1). That includes nearby file cabinets, end tables, the bulletin board behind your seat, and bookshelves. Even the ceiling can be a space to hang items.

NOT ALL DESKS ARE CREATED EQUAL

As for the desk itself, choose one with file drawer space, not one that just looks cool. A high school math teacher from Minneapolis adopted the *Miami Vice* look with a glass instructor's table. Not smart. In addition to having to be Windexed five times a day, it provided no storage, and its sharp corners bruised the teacher and students alike.

Figure 7.1 The instructor's desk should contain everything you need within reach.
Source: Image by Finley & Wiggs.

DESK PLACEMENT

Locate your desk in a place that affords you an unobstructed view of every-thing in the room and hallway. Though many teachers position their desk to the right or left of the chalkboard at the front of the room, the back of the room affords several advantages. Forward-facing students won't be able to calculate when to pass the notes or secretly cause a disruption without turning around to see if you are watching—a maneuver that telegraphs their intent.

DECLUTTER TRICKS

You can mitigate the visual mess of clutter by "hiding" a short table or bookshelf behind your desk. Also, spray paint baskets, trays, pen holders, DIY storage, and desk lamps the same color to give your desk the minimalist look.

DESK ITEM LIST

So, what goes in, on, or near the teacher's desk? The short answer is, *only the things you'll use often,* which may include some of the following:

- Minifridge
- Monday–Friday files (lessons and materials)
- Administrative paperwork:
  - bell schedule
  - class roll
  - attendance
  - school policies
  - in-school suspension writeups
  - hall, office, and bathroom passes
  - curriculum standards
  - handouts from faculty meetings, department meetings, and professional development
  - lunch menu
  - emergency procedures
  - lesson plans
  - discipline plan
  - parent contact information
  - schedule of teacher duties
  - birthday list

- student inventory checklist
- take-home folders
- classroom jobs
- checkout list for class library
- First aid kit: first aid guidebook, aspirin, bandages, tape, oval eye pad, scissors, tweezers, instant cold pack, disposable gloves, finger splint, gauze, safety pin, butterfly closures, antibiotic ointment, eye wash, CPR shield, and antacid
- Personal items: Hand sanitizer or antibacterial hand wipes, hand cream, mouthwash, gum, toothpaste (we recommend Arm & Hammer Extreme Whitening for coffee stains) and a toothbrush, eye-drops, ear plugs, a coffee mug, and tea bags
- Date stamp
- Stickers
- Pen drive
- Glue stick
- Hole punch / three-hole punch
- Scissors
- Chargers
- Legal pad
- Letter opener
- Wire stand-up file holder racks
- Clock
- Tablet stand
- Highlighter
- Binder clips
- Stikki clips
- Labeler
- Labels
- Envelopes
- Staples
- Storage clipboard
- Hanging files
- Charger stand
- Wire step file
- Desk pad
- Desktop calendar
- Paper clips and holder
- Rolodex®
- Pens, pencils, markers
- Pencil sharpener
- Erasers

- Angled telephone stand
- Rubber bands
- Scotch® tape dispenser and tape
- Lee Sortkwik® Hygienic Fingertip Moistener
- Ruler
- Calculator
- Snacks
- Correction fluid
- Bookends
- Palmrest and trackpad (for computing)
- Desktop trays
- Memos and memo holder
- Drawer organizer
- Letter tray
- Document holder

The blog *Eat.Write.Teach.* recommends that you obtain two sets of items that both you and the students need, such as staplers, scissors, tape, glue sticks, and hole punch. Your set stays on the desk while the other is placed in a student supply center away from the teacher's desk. "I try to get supplies that look different from my own and from day one I make it very clear that the supplies in front of the room are theirs to use and that they are not allowed to take any supplies from my desk."[1]

The following items will maximize your space near your desk:

- Trash can
- Shredder
- Floating shelves
- Fabric-covered bulletin board for notes, reminders, quotations, students' goals, and photos.
- Wall mount letter holder
- Message board or cork board
- Mobile of student photos or cards
- Paper slot mail sorters
- Stackable Sterilite translucent stacking bins

TIPS

The following ideas will help you maximize and organize your desk:

- Buy a Lazy Susan (rotating tray) to store often-used items on the desktop, such as hand soap, Stickies™, and paperclips.
- Trays will keep items from being scattered all over your desk.
- Instead of piling your technology-related cords on the desk or creating a pile of unsightly cords on the floor, use 3M™ sticky clips to keep your cords within reach underneath your main desk drawer.

DIY

You can do these projects on your own or involve students:

- *Pencil holders*—To make a pencil holder, Erin Loechner of *Design for Mankind* recommends gluing six cork trivets together, letting the adhesive harden overnight with a weight on top of the cork, and then drilling in pencil-accommodating holes using a ⅜-inch drill bit.
- *Recycle*—Laundry soap caps, mason jars, paint cans, and opened soup cans make great containers.
- *Eye-catching labels*—To make labels attractive and noticeable, buy letter stickers and seal them with Mod Podge® Acrylic Sealer.
- *Cheaper than fabric*—Buy an inexpensive or gently used sheet to use as a corkboard or bulletin board background.

ERGONOMICS

The Right Chair

To be comfortable and productive over an eight-hour period, choose a chair with adjustable arms, depth, and lumbar support. According to the Occupational Safety and Health Administration, your upper arms and elbows should be close to the body, wrists and hands straight, and thighs parallel to the floor. Your feet should rest flat on the floor or a footrest. Of the top ten office chairs recommended by Gear Patrol, only two are listed as below $200: the Office Star Air Grid and IKEA Markus.

Ergonomic Computing

Use a monitor arm to adjust the screen so that your eyes are level or below the top of the screen. Wrists should be flat and not resting on hard edges; purchase wrist pads if necessary. A wireless bluetooth keyboard and wireless mouse will also minimize cord clutter and are easily stowed off the desktop.

Workspace Alternatives

For a bit more shared space, you can always forgo a traditional teacher's desk by replacing it with a conference or kidney-shaped table for small group work. Hide supplies under the table by affixing a fabric skirt with VELCRO® Sticky Back Tape. Another option for teachers who rarely sit down during the school day is a small computer workstation and table.

Some educators create functional desks by setting a door on top of short bookshelves. Or to maximize floor space, you can purchase a floating wall desk; for an idea of what these look like, visit Orange22 Design Lab's website. And if you're wanting to take an even more radical step, you can follow English teacher Nicholas Provenzano's footsteps in high school. He ditched his desk for a whole year and enjoyed having more space for students.

FINAL THOUGHTS

Beyond students' impressions, how you organize your desk can influence the way administrators and colleagues view you as a professional. According to a CareerBuilder study, "Twenty-eight percent of employers say they are less likely to promote someone who has a disorganized or messy workspace."[2] So, what does your teacher's desk say about you?

Find more resources, images, and links related to this chapter at http://www. todd-finley.com/design-book-chapt-7-the-teachers-desk-conquering-clutter/.

NOTES

1. Richardson, S. (2013, July 2). Classroom Must-Haves for the First-Year Teacher. Retrieved June 26, 2015.

2. Huhman, H. (2011, September 16). 3 Reasons to Organize Your Workstation. *US News & World Report*. Retrieved June 26, 2015.

Chapter 8

Student Work

The Input-Output System

Nothing is less productive than to make more efficient what should
not be done at all.

—Pete Drucker

Guiding Questions

- How can you leverage technology to process student work?
- What are the five grading zones?
- How do you handle student makeup work?

LOTS OF STUFF

In today's climate, negotiating the frantic pace of teaching requires an airtight
system to handle the paper flow. Just think of all the "inputs" instructors have
to manage:

- Student essays
- Bulletins
- Professional journals
- Letters from parents
- Advertisements
- Letters of recommendation requests
- Club advisor paperwork
- Licensure update requests
- Professional development workshop materials

- PLN minutes and notes
- Class journals
- Behavior checklists
- Hall passes
- Attendance
- IEP meeting records
- Notes from student conferences
- Behavior contracts
- Professional organization communication
- Calendars
- Daily to-do checklists
- Catalogs
- Notes from parent-teacher conferences
- Performance reviews

When all the flat spaces above the floor in your classroom are covered with papers, the psychic RAM in your brain becomes overloaded. Disorganized classrooms are also a distraction to students. If your paper management system needs an overhaul, the next paragraphs are for you. Get ready to eliminate clutter, increase your productivity, and enhance student learning!

There are four ways to optimize paper flow:

1. *Clean up* messes.
2. *Process student work* more efficiently.
3. *Process all other "inputs"* by knowing what to do with paper that comes your way.
4. *Go paperless, go green*, and save time.

In the sections below, we'll discuss these four paper flow organizational strategies in more depth.

CLEAN UP

Everyone would like to wiggle their nose like the protagonist in *Bewitched* and make their classroom magically neat and organized. But ultimately, we're going to have to roll up our sleeves and go to work. However, you don't have to get it all done in a single day. In 2005, teacher Mike Newell decided that ten years of accumulated materials was making his classroom office uninhabitable. Here is his story:

The idea of spending two solid days deciding what to throw out, given my busy teaching schedule, seemed too daunting. But I remembered the story of Michel Lotito, a French entertainer who ate an entire Cessna 150 airplane! This was possible because Lotito broke the metal and other materials into small pieces, drank a lot of water and mineral oil (to line his intestine), and limited himself to eating 1 kilogram a day—equivalent to a large dictionary or pineapple.[1] This extraordinary feat illustrated for me the importance of breaking overwhelming tasks into bite-sized ones.

The following Monday, I brought two boxes of Glad ForceFlex garbage bags to my school. I like that brand because the bags have a diamond texture that stretches to prevent rips—necessary when you are throwing away folders, books, and other inorganic items. Deciding to make a little progress every day before school started, I arrived 15 minutes early to school every day and removed two trash bags full of stuff I no longer needed.

I estimated that the job would take about a week—emptying 2 bags a day. But it took me six weeks to remove 60 thirty-gallon bags of junk. The effort exerted was minimal. The effect, meanwhile was so liberating. Anyone can eat an airplane!

Getting Started

As Mike Newell's story illustrates, you don't have to do everything at once. However, if you want to remove all the junk in your classroom in one marathon purge-a-palooza, you'll need three trash bins: one for trash, one for recycling, and one for storage. Also, buy some quart-sized Ziploc™ bags, surgical gloves to save your hands from wear and tear, all-purpose cleaner, and rags.

Divide your room into four quadrants. Methodically look at every shelf, surface, drawer, and storage container in the first quadrant. Use one garbage bin for trash, the other for recycling and/or donation, and the third for items that you'll store off site. Assess each item: if it hasn't been used in five to six months, chuck it in one of your bins. When you finish one quadrant, move to the second, then third, and fourth.

What about that drawer full of cards, signed school playbills, photos, and artwork from former students? If you're overcome with nostalgia, take a photo of each item with your smartphone, then throw away the physical versions. You can upload all those photos to Evernote or Flickr where they can be viewed to your heart's content.

Purge with conviction. You don't need seven highlighters, and five Sharpie® pens.

Nor do you need eight canvas bags from conferences. Throw out that dehydrated Picante Beef Ramen. Pitch those proprietary USB cables into the trash. You don't need four coffee mugs. You need only one.

There is one special case. For items used only a couple of times a year that nevertheless fulfill an important classroom role, Jason Fitzpatrick's *Life-hacker* article recommends the following:

> We all have the odd cable we only use now and then for syncing this device or that and replacing it would be a huge pain. This is where the Ziploc™ bags come into play. Even if it would only cost $5 to replace the cable, the hassle of finding it online, ordering it, and waiting for it far outweighs the small amount of space the properly labeled and stored cable will take up. Put it in the Ziploc™ bag and label it clearly like "Panasonic Camcorder Cam-to-Composite AV Cable" to avoid any future "What is this?" moments during future cleaning sessions.[2]

PROCESS STUDENT PAPERWORK AND HANDOUTS

There are a variety of different containers you can use for organizing and storing materials:

- paper trays or stacking letter trays
- wall files
- file folders or hanging file folders
- file totes
- baskets
- tubs
- expanding files
- expanding file carriers
- pouches
- office sorters
- drawers
- portable file totes
- plastic or wood crates
- cubbies
- traditional yard mailboxes
- cupboards
- translucent document cases
- accordion files
- cascading (hanging) paper file totes
- mesh pouches
- vertical file holders
- stackable desktop drawers
- cereal boxes (Kellogg's Frosted Flakes cereal comes in a massive 61.9-ounce box on Amazon)
- printer paper boxes (or just the lids)

We recommend that you use a different color for each period or simply label each storage solution with the class period number. *The Clutter Free Classroom* recommends that you buy white and black containers or paint your containers those two colors: "The black matches so many classroom color schemes and can be used year after year even if you decide you want to change said color scheme" when doing a "classroom makeover in the future."[3]

Managing Student Paperwork

The most organized classrooms have five different places to store and manage student work, as shown in Figure 8.1.

The *student work submission zone* is the place for students to submit work that is due. You can save time by assigning each student a period and a number: *John Smith 103* (this number refers to period #1, student #3). When a class turns in a batch of papers, have an assigned student paper collector do the following:

- collect each paper, making sure all papers are facing up with the heading on top
- sort papers in numerical order
- check to make sure each submitted paper has the proper heading
- attach a cover sheet with the name of the assignment, the class period, the date the assignment was due, and the names of all the students in the class.

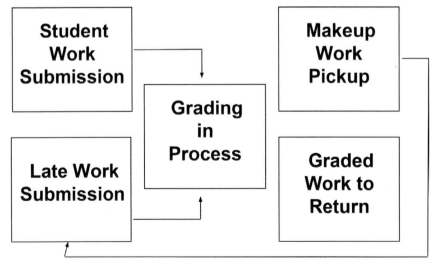

Figure 8.1   Five common student paperwork "zones." *Source*: Image by Finley & Wiggs.

- indicate which papers have been turned in and which ones have not on the cover sheet
- place the paper in the *work submission zone*

The *late work submission zone* is the place for absent students to submit work when they return to school. If you have a zone and procedure for dealing with late materials, then it's less likely that students will stack random papers on your desk. If you have an increasing penalty for work not turned in on time, we recommend that you empty this container every day, using a date stamp to indicate what time the assignment was received. Some teachers require that each late assignment has a completed "late work cover sheet" attached that includes the following prompts:

- Name:
- Period:
- Original due date:
- Date and time the work was submitted:
- Explain why the assignment was late:
- Would you like to arrange a time to receive more help on this assignment? Yes ___ No ___
- I understand that late assignments are docked [% or points]. Student signature: _____.

While scoring work, keep all assignments in the *grading in process zone*, preferably in some kind of file, tub, or portable translucent tote that keeps papers visible, together, and dry until you have entered all the grades into your gradebook. An anonymous teacher and author of *Tips for Teachers*, however, skips a step:

> I have gotten to the point where I no longer move the papers from the turn in baskets to the plastic drawers [her previous grading zone]. I simply take the work out of the baskets and grade them immediately at the end of the day, or stick them in my bag to grade at home or at the doctor's office or so on.[4]

The *makeup work pickup zone* is a place for absent students to collect makeup work directions and handouts. Have those pupils record what they have collected on a form next to the handouts—all organized by date. A middle school teacher in Massachusetts keeps his makeup work handouts in a bin with folders labeled for each day of the previous and current month. Next to the bin is a "What you Missed" log for each class that a student fills out with the following information:

- Topics that were covered in an outline format
- Names of each handout distributed
- Due dates discussed

If students miss a test, they have to sign up for a quiz makeup time.

Another way of reinforcing expectations is to hang a whiteboard on the wall behind the *makeup work pickup zone*. Every time a graded assignment is announced, the name and due date are posted in chronological order for the entire semester. We recommend that you add a check mark by those assignments that have been collected, graded, and returned.

The *graded work to return zone* is where scored assignments are placed after they have been entered into the gradebook. In this area, we recommend that you keep two file boxes, as shown in Figure 8.2.

The first box, labeled "graded work to return," should have file folders divided by class period for a volunteer to return to students. A slower approach involves inserting graded work in file folders that are individually numbered for each learner and color-coded by period.

The second box, labeled "graded and rogue papers (needing a home!)," should contain a file folder for every student you teach organized by period (e.g., red is first period and yellow is second period). Each file should be

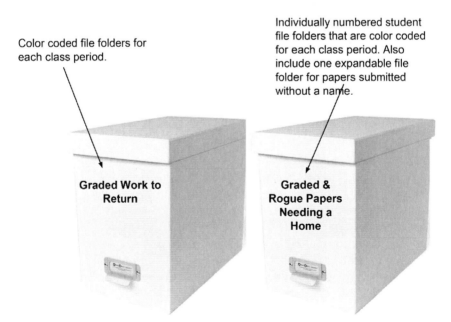

Figure 8.2 The Graded Work to Return Zone is where graded work goes after it has been entered into the gradebook. *Source*: Image by Finley & Wiggs.

labeled with a student name and number, in numerical order. Papers not returned because a student was absent can be inserted into the specific learner's folder. Keep another expandable file folder for papers turned in without a name—what we call "rogues."

Ruth Arseneault, a high school English teacher in New Brunswick, Canada, described to us how she processes student papers:

> When I collect student work, I have each student hand the assignment in, one by one, and I check them off on a cover sheet that lists each student for that period. If a student is absent, they are supposed to turn it in the next day, but they are supposed to put it in my hand so that I can tick it off and they are assured I got it. So students don't play that little trick.
>
> I use a big plastic paper clip to keep all the assignments together in a color-coded file for each class. The same file color is used each year for the same period, so I know that period 1 is always in a yellow folder. The checklist goes in the folder with all the work.
>
> When processing student work, I only record the grade on that same cover sheet. After that task is completed, I enter grades from those cover sheets into the grade program on my computer. Then I insert the cover sheet in a folder as backup in case my computer crashes.

Homework Folder

Finally, "Jennifer" offers a tip for how to manage homework in *The Teachers Corner*. Her students decorate their own oversized envelope with a clasp, which is processed through a laminator. "Everyone knows that when there is something to go home, we put it by the 'Friday Folder' stack for a volunteer student to file." Jennifer reports that no important projects have been lost since they implemented this system.[5]

PROCESS OTHER "INPUTS"

Even taking student work out of the equation, the amount of paperwork a teacher needs to handle each year would, with a lit match, make a mighty bonfire. Fortunately, the science of managing "inputs" has advanced because of books like David Allen's *Getting Things Done* and Tim Ferriss's *The 4-Hour Workweek*. These experts discuss how to leverage knowledge worker tools like calendars, file folders, and to-do lists—both physical and digital versions. The goal is to stay on top of your responsibilities so that you aren't waiting in line at the copy machine behind four other teachers thirty seconds before your class starts.

Here are some basic tactics for handling learning materials, not including student-produced assignments:

- Always make copies the day or night before class.
- Review your checklist every Friday to make sure you have accomplished critical tasks for the week.
- If you haven't used a lesson, handout (or any paper), or book for over twelve months, donate it or recycle the item. Freecycle.org and Paperbackswap.com can help with the recycling.
- Create a specific location for the following:
Handouts needing to be copied.
Copies of handouts and materials ready to be used.
Handouts and materials that have been used and are ready to be filed for use in a future class.
- File papers a minimum of every two weeks.

To see a representation of how to process all items that come your way, see Figure 8.3. The system can apply to physical items (memos and forms) and digital documents, like email. The key is to make quick decisions about where the input should be directed.

THE PAPERLESS CLASSROOM

With consistent wifi and an adequate number of student computers, it's now possible for many teachers to go paperless. In fact, several learning

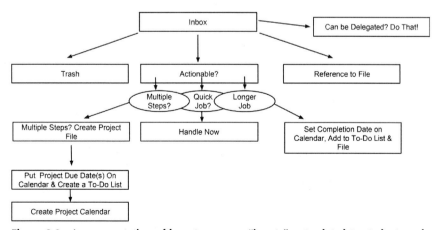

Figure 8.3 A representation of how to process "inputs" not related to student work.
Source: Image by Finley & Wiggs.

management systems (LMSs) make this process intuitive. As of this writing, the five most popular LMSs are the following:

- Moodle (71 million users)
- SuccessFactor (28 million users)
- Blackboard (20 million users)
- SkillSoft (19 million users)[6]

Edmodo, with 49 million users, would make the list, but its developers insist that Edmodo is not an LMS; they call it a "teacher-centered social learning platform." Regardless, all those platforms, including Edmodo, make it easy for student work to be stored and graded in the cloud.

Vicki Davis, a teacher in Georgia and author of the *Cool Cat Teacher* blog, described to us how she manages student work. Students submit digital work to Dropbox.com, a cloud-based home for multiple types of files that syncs between devices and makes it easy for students to share work with teachers and for the teachers to grade right in the Dropbox folder.

Davis uses SortMyBox.com, which employs rules similar to email filters to automatically move files to specific locations. So, when a student submits work to the "turn in" folder to be graded, SortMyBox.com instantly inserts the document into a "to grade" folder where only Davis can see it.

We have found Evernote—a cloud-based note-taking and archiving tool— to be invaluable for storing and retrieving planning material: articles, photos, videos, and other documents. Also, the tool easily houses student portfolios that the teacher can comment upon.

A QUICK NOTE ABOUT EMAIL

Although dealing with email is beyond the scope of this guide, we realize that managing your digital inbox consumes valuable time and energy. We, therefore, recommend *Lifehacker: The Guide to Working Smarter, Faster, and Better*, by Adam Pash and Gina Trapani. The book's chapter on "Controlling Your Email" is available as a free sample chapter (www.lifehackerbook. com).

FINAL THOUGHTS

We all know that an organized classroom space can increase productivity.[7] But improving paper management won't occur unless you (a) are honest about the true state of your paperwork system, (b) set goals, and (c) process paper through your system every day.

Find more resources, images, and links related to this chapter at http://www. todd-finley.com/design-book-chapt-8-student-work-the-input-output-system/.

NOTES

1. Lorenzo, T. (2012, October 1). *Michel Lotito: The Man Who Ate an Airplane And Everything Else*. Retrieved June 26, 2015.

2. Fitzpatrick, J. (2010, June 11). *The End-All Guide to Getting Out from Under Your Office Crap*. Retrieved June 26, 2015.

3. Clutter-Free Classroom Guide to Organizing & Managing Your Classroom. (2013). Retrieved June 7, 2015, from https://www.teacherspayteachers.com/Product/Clutter-Free-Classroom-Guide-to-Organizing-Managing-Your-Classroom-119900.

4. Getting Organized—Mandy's Tips for Teachers! (2011). Retrieved June 7, 2015, from http://www.tips-for-teachers.com/gettingorganized.htm.

5. Teacher Resources and Classroom Management. (2010). Retrieved June 10, 2015, from http://www.theteacherscorner.net/teacher-resources/teachhelp.php.

6. Best LMS (Learning Management System) Software. (2014). Retrieved June 10, 2015, from http://www.capterra.com/learning-management-system-software/.

7. Stronge, J., Tucker, P., & Hindman, J. (2004). Chapter 3. Classroom Management and Organization. In *Handbook for Qualities of Effective Teachers*. Alexandria, VA: Association for Supervision and Curriculum Development.

Chapter 9

Concluding Thoughts

The philosophy of the school room in one generation will be the philosophy of government in the next.

—Abraham Lincoln

Guiding Questions

- What is the future of classroom design?
- Whose voices do we need to include for education reform to succeed?

WE NEED MORE MAKERS

The National Writing Project's executive director, Elyse Eidman-Aadahl, envisions classrooms that go beyond standardized test preparation. "School should be the engine for creativity and curiosity and taking risks. These are the kids who are going to have to solve global warming, to work in jobs that don't exist yet."

What kind of classroom design supports Eidman-Aadahl's vision to foster student agency and create a generation of problem-solvers?

We believe that the future of classroom design is embodied in the Maker movement, which engages students in problem-solving tasks. Echoing many of the principles of the Do It Yourself (DIY), FabLab, and Hackerspace movements, "Makerspace grew out of Maker Media, the force behind MAKE magazine and Maker Faire and a leader in the Maker movement."[1]

In terms of design, this approach rejects the traditional straight-row classroom model where students receive content from lectures and textbooks.

Instead of acting as consumers of knowledge, Makerspaces invite students to help produce the content and curriculum and solve real problems now, rather than waiting until they graduate.

We are writing this chapter after just visiting a vibrant Makerspace at Rose High School (see Figure 9.1) where a dozen high school faculty from different disciplines gather in a library to learn the principles of design thinking from professor Stephanie West-Puckett and teaching coach Mike Flinchbaugh.

Together, they are planning different Makerspace labs to occur during the high school's flex time: upcycling, music, prototype fabrication, fashion, and others. But here's the kicker: the Maker planning group asked fifteen high school students to help choose and develop the labs. Furthermore, those fifteen learners will help fellow students follow their affinities by leading the Maker labs with their instructors in fall.

"The reason why most school reform is unsuccessful is because the planners failed to consult with the students," West-Puckett explained.

Youths will need skills to solve the water shortage problem, human rights issues, and space exploration. Therefore, the classrooms where they internalize critical thinking, empathy, disciplinary knowledge, and can-do attitudes should be pretty awesome. Since classrooms are ostensibly designed for *students'* benefit, we subscribe to another big idea of Makerspaces: we should also invite students to help rethink and redesign classrooms spaces.

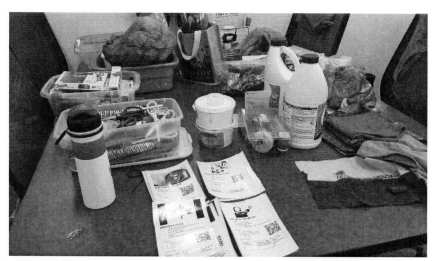

Figure 9.1 Materials from a Makerspace that focuses on upcycling fabric. Upcycling converts discarded materials into useful and aesthetically pleasing artifacts. At the forefront of the image, challenge cards with QR codes are provided to students in each lab to get them started. *Source*: Image by Finley & Wiggs.

Find more resources, images, and links related to this chapter at http://www.todd-finley.com/design-book-chapt-9-concluding-thoughts-what-is-the-future-of-classroom-design/.

NOTE

1. *Makerspace Playbook* (School ed.). (2013). Maker Media. Retrieved from http://makered.org/wp-content/uploads/2014/09/Makerspace-Playbook-Feb-2013.pdf.

Index

About the Authors

Todd Finley, PhD, is a tenured professor of English Education at East Carolina University. He has taught elementary and 7th–12th grade English and codeveloped the Tar River Writing Project. His BA in Elementary Education and Secondary English was earned at the University of Puget Sound. His MA in English and PhD in Curriculum and Instruction were earned at the University of Minnesota.

An education generalist with special expertise in composition pedagogy and technology, he has published in national and regional peer-reviewed journals, has keynoted and presented at national and regional conferences, and has been a panelist and presenter on podcasts and webinars. He blogs and is an assistant editor for Edutopia (George Lucas Foundation).

Blake Wiggs received both his BA in Anthropology and MA in Teaching from East Carolina University. He is a School Reform Initiative (SRI) facilitator and a teacher-consultant with the National Writing Project. Over the course of his teaching career, he has presented in various academic venues relating to cross-curricular mapping, hybrid/online learning communities, global awareness, teaching tolerance, and social justice education.

Blake Wiggs is currently working as an instructional coach with NC New Schools/Breakthrough Learning and enjoys hosting make-believe tea parties, painting fingernails, and performing impromptu finger puppet shows with his wife and daughter at their home in New Bern, North Carolina.